ENEMY
OF THE
HUMAN
RACE

HATE IS A SPIRIT. HATE IS UGLY.
HATE PLACES NO VALUE ON HUMAN LIFE.

DR. HENRY I. BALOGUN

LifeRich PUBLISHING®

This book is a work of non-fiction. Unless otherwise noted, the author and the publisher make no explicit guarantees as to the accuracy of the information contained in this book and in some cases, names of people and places have been altered to protect their privacy.

LifeRich Publishing is a registered trademark of The Reader's Digest Association, Inc.

LifeRich Publishing books may be ordered through booksellers or by contacting:

LifeRich Publishing
1663 Liberty Drive
Bloomington, IN 47403
www.liferichpublishing.com
1 (888) 238-8637

Because of the dynamic nature of the Internet, any web addresses or links contained in this book may have changed since publication and may no longer be valid. The views expressed in this work are solely those of the author and do not necessarily reflect the views of the publisher, and the publisher hereby disclaims any responsibility for them.

Any people depicted in stock imagery provided by Getty Images are models, and such images are being used for illustrative purposes only.
Certain stock imagery © Getty Images.

Scripture taken from the King James Version of the Bible.

ISBN: 978-1-4897-2478-6 (sc)
ISBN: 978-1-4897-2477-9 (hc)
ISBN: 978-1-4897-2476-2 (e)

Library of Congress Control Number: 2019912863

Print information available on the last page.

LifeRich Publishing rev. date: 09/11/2019

Our world is seeded with landmine of hate, moral
deficiencies, inequalities and collaboration with evil

The greatest enemy of the human race; a major roadblock to
genuine integration, equality, and peaceful coexistence is
hate and the spread of it.

This book takes a deeper look at hate, only to stumble on the real collusion with regard to the election of 2016. The truth is hereby revealed; and the culprit, the man behind it all, is exposed.

Please understand that all references to the Scripture cited in this book are from the King James Version of the Bible

CONTENTS

ACKNOWLEDGMENTS

In spite of unspeakable chaos, political, religious, philosophical, and otherwise, including nonchalant and carefree attitude toward one another, our world is, no doubt, full of many angels of light, those who just like to brighten somebody's day by their knowledge, talent, job performance, and how they interact with other members of the human family including how they react to the less fortunate. These are the people who refused to cooperate with evil by subscribing to what is good, honorable, and uplifting. This is not something they struggle with or are forced to do; it comes natural to them. They are the few who have decided to be coworkers with God no matter what.

My sincere gratitude to many whose lifelong devotion to justice, equality, and peaceful coexistence makes it possible for all of God's children to wake up in the morning feeling good about themselves. Those who refused to allow negative energy to emanate through them. Those who refused to participate in the idea of making life of the innocent miserable and completely impossible through willful desire of inflicting pain in the interest of political agenda, religious differences, greed, nationalistic agenda including self-righteous desire deeply rooted and grounded in arrogant, delusional, and un-Christian-like idea of "You are beneath me" or "This is our street, this is our city."

Those who decided to not allow illegal injunctions designed to silence and take away the "right to protest for rights." Those who gave up pleasure of the moment in the interest of making sure the shut-ins, the hungry, the weak, and the disadvantaged are not forgotten.

How can I forget those who gave up one day, one week, or one month of their entire life to combat evil anywhere they see one? Those who will not stop fighting for those who cannot fight for themselves! Those, in the words of Dr. King: "whose voices are yet unheard, whose course is yet unclear, and whose courageous acts are yet unseen."

As the scripture says, "Be ye steadfast, unmovable, always abounding in the work of the Lord, forasmuch as ye know that your labor is not in vain in the Lord"

REVIEWERS FEEDBACK

Few books I have read were at the exact moment I needed to read them. This is one of them.

The more I read, the more I felt this book was not only a nonfiction book about politics to an extent, it was a self help book, it was a book on spirituality, above all, it was a book that made me think which I always strive for.

What an important book when the world could use more love.

Kathleen T

I really enjoyed reading this book and I would definitely look into reading more books by this author.

A.D.

It took me a while to read this book because how the author explores hate, injustice, anger, and destruction needs utmost patience. It's not the kind of book you'd read in a sitting and it reminded me of a conversational book. The kind that you can read a section of it and start a discussion on major life changing aspects!

Dora Archie O,

This book is so good! It's thought provoking, and blisteringly critical of the current culture of hate that is raging through the US. It at once shines a light on the degrading nature of hate in our culture and inspires the readers to do better.

Chantell R,

It is hate in its many forms (pride, greed, abuse) that will destroy the human race. While hate grows and is written off or simply ignored, populism grows that brings forth leaders interested in feeding the fears of others. "When the man of God is no longer the man of God, politics and secular teachings creep in—morality, the truth, and the power of prayer takes the backseat. The church then becomes almost like a club of like-minded people but still retains the appearance of the house of God."

Hate grows when fears, false history, racial superiority, and messages go unchallenged. Hate expands when leaders use these fears as a form of populism and capitalize on amplifying the same hatred. Lies are repeated so many times without shame that they are accepted as truth. Even religion is not spared in Balogun's fiery and fact-filled presentation. Enemy of the Human Race is a book that cuts deep into the problem of hate and its methods. It does more than describe the problem; it presents a cure.

This book is very unique in its message and tone. The fiery tone works well with the message and tying religion, Christianity, into the message should appeal to a large portion of the population. Also, the use of Christianity seems almost weaponized to fight hate.

International review of books

INTRODUCTION

Our world is full of hostilities partly inherited and partly grounded and rooted in heresy. The legacy of history presumed to be credible but carefully crafted, manipulated, twisted, and presented to those whose minds are itching for something different cannot be ignored. Looking for accurate portrayal of history is like looking for gold in the same spot that was excavated and almost completely extracted and exhausted. The hope of finding more is not lost, and the possibility of hitting another and similar amount of hiding treasure as was originally found is very much greater than zero. However, you may have to continue to dig your way through an area that is completely bare, with no treasure of any kind, even though the person behind the misleading detour is not unaware of their deception and conniving intent.

History had gone through many erroneous and self-serving modifications and editing in the interest of creating alternative version wholly responsible for the damaging, divisive, and extraordinarily hateful world we are living in. The damaging version of history we are left with is extremely toxic. Peaceful coexistence demand that we act swiftly and embark on what is dignified, promote better interactions to stop further division and, eventually, annihilation.

If all I have to establish the truth is individual opinion or interpretation, the purpose of writing about the forgotten part of history is dead on arrival. It is, no doubt, highly required of me to give you authentic blueprint that was ignored by all organizations and historians until now. I had to dig deeper to expose the real enemy of the human family—hate and misinformation!

"If we continue to encourage supremacy and the current false sense of ascendancy in the interest of self-magnification and control, the future is uncertain." Many of the dysfunction in our world has never been fully addressed and dealt with due to the fact that "privileged group seldom give up their privileges voluntarily without some resistance."

What you believed to be the authentic story of the past depends on how plausible the story you are provided with in light of your own ideological point of view, and how willing you are to hold that version as the truth. History, like onions, has many layers; and it depends on the layer you are left to grapple with. It is not uncommon to suppress the truth in favor of what is preferred and believed should be released to the world.

There was that version of history from centuries ago—although recorded, suppressed, but never destroyed. It no doubt was regarded as old history that was never allowed to see the light of day. These are regarded as the innermost layers of the onion analogy. Next are those extracted from the original version only to be rearranged and manipulated. These represent the middle layers. However, the outer layers are the most recent—a mixture of the manipulated, controlled, and diluted history. They are presented as the only authentic historical version. Somehow, they managed to magnify these outer layers, through deception, and gave it to the world as the ultimate truth. What a shame!

This book is written to reveal what was real and true including where did what is declared actually took place. It gives you those who were involved, looking at what happened to whom and by whom. It is also written to discredit false assumption and baseless better-than-them-attitude, which is the bedrock of supremacy as we know it today. Those who were robbed of what was rightfully theirs believe that the carefully concocted history they are left with is their true and authentic history. Not only were they deliberately misled, they were lampooned and ridiculed for their willingness to follow blindly and also for their gullibility. Perpetrators believed that the truth, buried and never to be revealed, are going to remain buried forever. Nothing could be further from the truth!

It is amazing that manipulated history intentionally designed to marginalize an entire ethnic group disregard their feelings while trampling on their dignity including their all-important contributions to civilization, and growth had always been music to the ears of supremacists all over the world. Whatever iota of inclusiveness experienced by some members of this forgotten group quickly gave way to many unscientific and extremely dehumanizing assumptions. The privileged few came up with smear tactics of "less than" in every aspect of life—"less intelligent," "less human" (which was characterized as "subhuman"), "less concerned," "less aware of their rightful place in the world," and "less appreciative of what was given to them by God."

Without doubt, greed, fear, intimidation, and segregation engineered by misinformation and solidified by unsolicited, bias, and destructive studies coupled with extraordinary fear of the disadvantaged along with unspeakable display of emotional reactions of the privileged few entered our world and we have never been the same.

How was it so possible to suppress the truth through carefully crafted and concocted approach designed to deceive the whole world into believing lies and innuendos to the exclusive neglect of the truth including all references to facts and all that was legally and intellectually available? What kind of explanation, if any, to support inexplicable invasion of the mind of those who could have asked that we take a careful look at every action pointing to the truth? If what was revealed about "slavery" was true and all Africans in Americas fell into that degrading category back in the 16th to 18th centuries ago, where did the vast ocean of information available to prove otherwise come from? Where did that other information that were never explored and still available in the hand of the United States government and now available in the public domain come from?

Blindly following and trusting has not produced any helpful, healthy equality of interactions but extremely divisive and arrogant attitude of "We are ordained to rule the world" mind-set. They are also under the impression that they are divinely predestined by God, thereby should control the destination of others and dictate to them how they should live their lives. This is the source of the destructive sense of superiority and supremacy we are now wrestling with.

The fact that the main bone of contention, which is suppressed information and misinformation, was never addressed and dealt with had led to the reemergence of concealed hate, which is like cancer in our world. The status quo believes in convincing the disadvantaged that a do-nothing-but-wait-patiently-strategy that is self-serving with nothing beneficial to anyone is the answer. Most people are left to wrestle with deep-seated unresolved emotional issues that present no solution but a time bomb just waiting to explode.

This book does not believe in scratching the surface. If you are looking for pacifier or possibly vaporizer, you may be disappointed. The need to dig deeper in the interest of peaceful coexistence demand that we address without sugarcoating the truth and get to the heart of division as much as humanly possible! It also demands that we look back into what got us where we are. By the same token, this book also takes a leap forward without fear. The search for solutions demands it. The desire to end segregation, divisiveness, and hate demands it. Above all, the hope of seeing the human family come together as one demands it.

If anyone is hoping to see the truth buried through intimidation and threat, that someone or group might be disappointed because the need for a better approach dictate that the truth must be told. "We are immortal until the work is done."

The focus in this volume is on revealing the greatest enemy of the human race—hate. Hate is everywhere and in all of our interaction with one another. Hate in religion is revealed. Hate in politics is discussed. Many facets of hate are fully exposed without hesitation. The role of misinformation and misnomer in conjunction with the apathy and indifference of politicians, and those who believe they are Christians are not left out.

No doubt, hate is at the center of our discord and is the main reason behind the unspeakable gulf of division in the world. Hate, by and large, is the most potent enemy of mankind. Hate is not something that can be scrubbed out or washed away with whatever. Hate is to the devil what the Holy Spirit is to God. Holy Spirit is available and ready to activate all the attributes of God within any willing member of the human family.

While the Holy Spirit is ready to activate "whatsoever things are honest, whatsoever things are just, whatsoever things are pure, whatsoever things are lovely, whatsoever things are of good report," including things that are of virtue and worthy of praise, hate is also available and ready to activate all those things that are opposite and working against.

Hate can be seen in every aspect of human life. As much as some of us would have loved to pretend, the truth is difficult to defeat. There is hate in religion, and if you care to look, you would find it in the most religious organization's foundation, constitution, and tenet. There is hate in politics. History had proven time and again that there is no better place to promote and propagate hate than politics. Those who represent you would like to make you believe otherwise, but if you take a careful look, you would discover the truth for yourself. What about government? The presence of hate cannot be mistaken for something else. It is capable of making itself known even when we are too naive or too trusting to suspect.

Hate is always interrupting and always disrupting. It is capable of wiping away smiles and activating tears without warning. It does not matter who is affected—young, old, innocent babies, including those who (for no fault of their own) found themselves in degrading predicaments. Hate does not believe in entitlement and certainly not in lending a helping hand. It does not matter if you have spent your entire life helping humanity, hate is not considerate. Hate is there to let you know that you are on your own.

Any discussions or exposé about hate will be incomplete without a brief look at the role of anger. Without anger, hate is powerless. Anger is the driving force, the propelling power of hate. Anger is the energizing boost ready to push hate to its apex. On the flip side, anger also stands at the intersection of good and evil, ready to work against or in favor. How is this possible?

Anger is required to effectively deal with hate. If your anger level is suppressed, it will turn you into a person not better than a zombie. If your anger is devoid of knowledge and the best way to demand your right, you are on the road to becoming a menace to society. You have to be angry enough to want to know what happened in the past. You have to be angry enough to stand up and say those things that set us against one another cannot be allowed to continue. You have to be angry enough to be able to see the unprecedented effect of division brought about by hate. This is why the Bible encourages anger: "Be angry, but let not the sun go down on your anger." Mental health professionals have not been able to come up with cure for anger because there is none. You just have to know how to manage yours.

Hate respects no one, fears no one, and not interested in looking for what is good or be concerned about human feelings or level of achievement. Hate will destroy hopes and dreams without blinking and without remorse. You cannot afford to not stand up against hate. If you resign to fate or the drumbeat of those asking you to relax, you, your children, as well as many generations to come are going to be the beneficiaries of devastating inaction.

The hope of escaping tyranny, oppression, religious persecution, and injustice is about to go through unprecedented rude awakening. The enemy within is a formidable one, not afraid to overtake, with intent to drastically deviate from the dictate of the constitution and the rule of law. The enemy within is not afraid to restructure and selfishly change the very fabric of the United States of America. An unprecedented hope of reviving hate is about to see the light of another day. Hate groups are pinning their hopes on the man who publicly declared, "I am your voice." With that said, they are coming out in record number.

This volume takes an in-depth look at hate in all its appearances. A full explanation of hate is provided. Further explanation is also provided to help us understand different faces of hate in all its transformation. It doesn't stop there! This volume carefully examines the footstep of man to expose what is actually going on. I invite you to take a careful look especially at the following:

- Politics—meddling in election with intent to distract for personal and national gain. It also includes implicit and explicit collusion carried out in plain sight. Who says there was no collusion? You've got to see the truth as it is carefully revealed here.
- The plan of the man who gained tremendously from the collusion itself is exposed along with some of his secret agenda and plan for the United States.
- Full description of *hate* as currently exists. The footprint of hate in our society along with different types of hate fully explained.

- What about
  - hate in religion and
  - hate in politics
- You will also get to know the entanglement between extremists and hate.
- The land established as the melting pot is not left out. What is going on in the land of "We the people"? See it for yourself in
  - "USA 2.0: The Revival of Hate"
  - "USA in the Age of Trump"
- You've got to see the man at the citadel of power—a would-be dictator who would have loved to change everything that makes the United States of America great, thereby transform it into a new totalitarian society. The question:
  - Who is Donald J. Trump? This book provides a glimpse, thereby answering the question a little differently.
- The unyielding spirit of those who stuck their necks out for what they believed is captured and explained.

We cannot overlook the following:

- Antonym of *hate*
- Finding our way back to the future, including consequences of inaction

Our world is, needless to say, suffering from unnecessary elevated temperature; and the only treatment option currently available is "nonviolence or nonexistence."

We cannot afford not to get it right. The future of the next generation depends on what we do today and where we go from here. What happened in the past, although seriously sad, ugly and highly destructive can be corrected. This is what matters now. Apathy and the feeling of "as long as I am not affected" will only make it possible for the evil spirit of hate to remain on the throne and continue to torment the human family.

We have to address the discord currently existing. If you have better information than presented here, do not hesitate to step forward. Intimidation and unnecessary threat of any kind from anyone will not work. Make time to read this book and the first book entitled *Culprit of Division* very carefully, step forward with whatever it is that you have, and let the discussions begin. Many children of God from the United States and around the world willing to stand against hate will continue to do so without fear.

DESTRUCTIVE SPIRIT

Hate is a spirit that can masquerade itself as innate acceptable behavior or unsuspecting cultural differences or bias. It is capable of taking on an appearance of human traits. It is very insidious and overpowering. It respects no one and devoid of consideration for human life. Dictionary defines *hate* as "intense or passionate dislike; extreme aversion or hostility." It can lead to ungodly feeling of irreconcilable prejudice, intolerance, and discrimination with no justification but baseless preferential choice such as "I just don't like them" or "I will do anything to avoid them" or be separated from them and have nothing to do with them but use them for our ultimate goal.

Hate is ugly. Hate does not understand empathy or sympathy. It is totally blind to the feeling of its intended target and highly insensitive to the suffering of others. Hate is illogical and always produce shocking, bewildering, unimaginable, and senseless outcome that cannot be rationalized or sensibly explained in a godly light. When one is engulfed with hate, consequential reasoning disappears and irrational justification takes over with a huge mess left behind for all caring souls to deal with. Every effort to explain the rationale behind hate can quickly give way to more irrational sense of pride and entitlement not built on facts but false assumptions. It can quickly escalate to a more irrational, unacceptable, and stupid behavior deserving the biggest backlash that can be unleashed without warning.

Hate places no value on human life. It brings about holier-than-thou attitude with extreme assumption of stupidity assigned to any opposing views or beliefs. Hate believes that the rule of law can be defeated by constantly looking for loophole and a way to justify the unjustifiable.

A hate-filled person cannot afford not to stay focused on his or her mission. There is always a better explanation for whatever decision is made. It does not matter if the decision is unpopular or illogical. It does not matter if the decision is theologically, socially, or politically unacceptable and wrong. A hate-filled person usually depends on the people around him or her, including supporters and surrogates to explain and thereby justify actions taken. Hate comes in different forms. Let us examine and reveal hate as currently exists

MISINTERPRETATION: SYNTAX ERROR

The word *hate* cannot be fully explained by focusing only on English meaning of hate. We have to step out and take a closer look at the meaning of *hate* in Hebrew and Greek. As per the interpretation provided by the King James Version of the scripture, it is a known fact that Jesus used the word *hate* in reference to what is required to follow Him. In the book of Luke 14:26, as revealed by King James Version, Jesus says, "If any man come to me, and hate not his father, and mother, and wife, and children, and brethren, and sisters, yea, and his own life also, he cannot be my disciple."

This interpretation, no doubt, set prerequisite for discipleship. However, something is missing. If the interpretation presented in English, is left the way it is; it, no doubt, misses the mark. We need to reach out to Hebrew and Greek languages to get it right. What Jesus was referring to in that chapter and verse is known in Hebrew as *sane*, which means "prefer over." or in Greek as *miseó*, which simply means "love less."

Sane is what was translated as *hate* in Luke 14:25–26 KJV. The same goes for *miseó*, the Greek word translated as *hate*. Without explanation, it looks like something disdainful with a strong appearance and connotation of dislike. Interpretation provided does not support deep "'psychological sense of anger or emotional desire to go against" with intent to destroy.

In Hebrew, the word *hate*, as used in the scripture, carries a meaning different from "vitriolic," "despised," or "detest." It simply means to "prefer over" or "love less." In explicit term, God did not leave room for ambiguity or any other interpretation. God made it crystal clear right from the beginning when he said, "I, the LORD your God, am a jealous God" (Exodus 20:5). Earlier in the same chapter within the same breath, He made it known when He said, "Thou shall have no other gods besides me" (Exodus 20:3). What Jesus said in Luke means you cannot "love" Him "less" than you love your father, mother, wife, children, brethren, sisters, including your own life. He was simply asking for greater love. Hebrew makes it much clearer when you look at the interpretation given to "hate" what God is saying is that thou shall not (sane) "prefer" any other god "over" Him. Jesus simply brought it to the human level when He said in a way that you cannot (sane) "prefer" father, mother, wife, children, brethren, sisters, and your own life *over* Him. Within the theological interpretations are the following:

PREFERENTIAL

This sometimes is true within a family. To love everyone the same way is what is expected and hoped for, but behavioral issues or choices made, or influences on or unrelated external stimuli, can lead to "sane" (prefer over) love. It does not, in any way, terminate relationship or relational love: "That's the way he is or she is, but I'm his or her mother until I die" or "He is the black sheep of the family, but I love him anyway."

Sibling rivalry or intrusion by a family member or unapproved use of what belongs to the other sibling can lead to the yelling of "I hate you." This is simply saying "I love you less right now for using my stuff without permission or for damaging that precious gift from Grandma." As a parent, I cannot tell you how many times I have heard the word *hate* used loosely without malice and without hostility but simply to say, "I love you less right now."

Preferential hate can, sometimes, lead to hoping for something better: "I am hoping for improvement and generally acceptable behavior or outlook on life." No matter how we wish this individual will conform to acceptable norm or expectation, at times, we have to accept whatever outcome, even if different from expectations or against tradition or the culture we grew up with. Preferential hate does not terminate and can never lead to concealed or gratuitous hate but would have loved to see a different outcome

It is perfectly okay to hate "prefer" a specific event "over" another such as watching football instead of baseball. To hate a choice or decision is not uncommon. You can even prefer that a family member marries someone of the same ethnic group as opposed to a person of different ethnic group—remember, we are all members of the same human race. They can even avoid being explicitly against a specific type of decision without being irrationally hostile, controlling, and evil.

CIRCUMSTANTIAL

It is not uncommon to hate a situation such as being compelled to do what you would not normally do: "You guys are going to make me do this?" You can express your resentment or hate of a specific circumstance without hostility. This in Hebrew is what "prefer over" hate is all about.

As much as God is able to do whatever He desires, He gave us free volition—freedom to choose, hence the clarion call to not "sane" (prefer over) Him or "miseo" (love Him less). Even if you prefer something else or prefer another god over Him or you love Him less, you can still bet on enjoying his goodness in the land of the living. You can still call on Him even in your darkest hour. He will not turn His back or say to you, "I knew you not." As much as we would like to believe that He had ordained some people to kill you in any way convenient for them, God still remains loving and merciful, who will not deviate from His word and promise. "Let God be true, but every man a liar" (Romans 3:4).

Hebrew's interpretation of *hate* provides clarity on the type of hate necessary for uprightness, acceptable interaction with fellow human being, and obedience to divine law. "Sane" is a necessary type of hate all God-fearing people should not be afraid to be equivocal about. You should not be afraid to come out against whatever your conscience tells you or the word of God declares as unacceptable such as injustice, division, religious persecution, and intolerance. Every God-loving and God-fearing individual should not be afraid to speak out against whatever they see as unacceptable: "I hate injustice," or "I hate brutality in any form," or "I hate violence, domestic or otherwise," or "I hate sexual interactions that is not mutually acceptable," or "I hate abuse in whatever form." In essence, what you are saying here is I "prefer" love "over" hate, or I "prefer" nonviolent resistance "over" destruction or unnecessary attack," or I "prefer" to accept my fellow members of the human raise "over" discrimination and ungodly prejudice.

In spite of the original intent of those before us based on what was allowed as a result of divine interactions, our world was about to be invaded in a way never before seen in history. In 1860, "delegates from South Carolina, Mississippi, Florida, Alabama, Georgia, and Louisiana convened in Montgomery, Alabama to establish the Confederate States of America." That gave birth to greater hate (concealed hate and gratuitous hate) and marked the beginning of division on a different and unique level in history. Concealed hate and gratuitous hate, which has been around in different forms and package, emerged! They turned our world upside down and quickly drowned out divine message of love and replaced it with fear, apathy, and intimidation.

CONCEALED HATE

"Overt or covert ill will." This and gratuitous form of hate are evil. However, concealed hate is the sneaky and the most difficult to detect. The person engulfed with concealed hate is usually difficult to please, and no amount of convincing or preaching is strong enough or makes sense enough to change them. No good deed, not even if ordained by God and established in the scripture, will make a difference. Once you are identified and targeted, they must deliver. Don't let anybody fool you; the weapons are going to be formed. The traps are going to be set. Lying in ambush to catch you can go on for years, if that's what it will take. The only protection and your only shield are with the Lord Himself.

Hate can take on subtle, welcoming, and friendly but deceitful persona with an appearance of something helpful, beneficial, and needful. Concealed hate is capable of delivering deadly venom strong enough to terminate life or destroy dreams and aspirations with a smile, without conscience, and without remorse or repentance.

Concealed hate can masquerade itself as politically and socially acceptable form of "prejudice" that most people are not ashamed to admit. They usually like to justify their action using phrases such as "I know I'm prejudiced and biased in my judgment on this subject, but how can you not be . . .?" Some of the things to remember about prejudice by a person or group of people with concealed hate is that it oftentimes operates on preconceived notions—a quiet weapon carefully crafted with intent to deny equal opportunities without making it too alarming, insult intelligence with unspeakable cruelty wrapped in one of the most enticing packages designed to give appearance of the truth, reject aspiration and effort, and disrespectful of those who are different in a way that is not explicitly obvious. Prejudice by a person or group of people with concealed hate can sometimes hide behind corporate policies, political ideology, ungodly religious constitution, tenet, or tradition.

There is a better chance for a black person aspiring to become the CEO of any of the largest corporations on the planet or becoming the pope or becoming the president of the United States or the prime minister of Britain than to become a senior pastor of a religious organization such as the Assemblies of God, Southern Baptist Union, or any of the so-called organized evangelical establishments unless that African American individual is the founder/senior pastor. What are the chances of an African American becoming a sponsored missionary to any country? It no doubt is close to none.

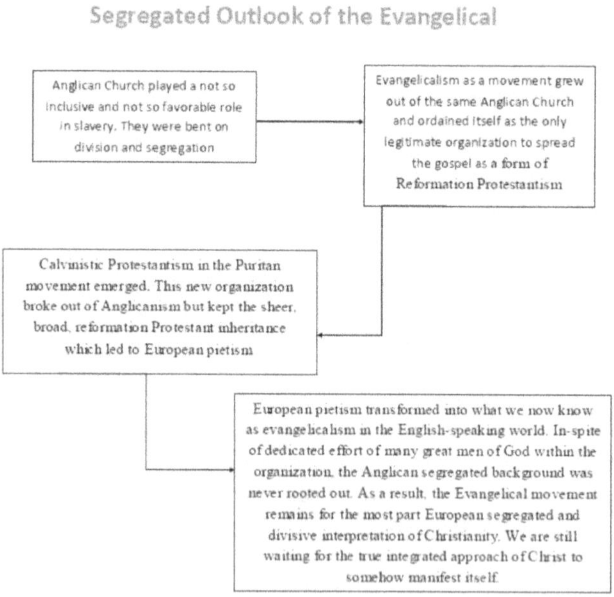

Segregated Outlook of the Evangelical

Figure 1: Inspired by history of the church

6

What about the Orthodox churches all over the world! The claim of the Orthodox churches as a regional religion provides unspeakable, appalling form of excuse and a reason for unjustifiable segregation and prejudice. Needless to say, it violates the divine call of a universal God whose love cannot be confined or intentionally segregated along language, culture or national origin. The clarion call of the gospel is "whosoever will, let him come."

There is absolutely no reason why children of God (black, white, or yellow) cannot be allowed to serve or be served in the house of God regardless of the color of their skin. Dr. King once called it appalling "that the most segregated hour of Christian America is eleven o'clock on Sunday morning." Any effort to justify segregation in the sanctuary, a place we call the house of God, is ungodly, antihuman, and evil.

Prejudice by a person or group of people with concealed hate oftentimes operate on erroneous assumption, unfounded fear and apprehension, blatant and unsubstantiated dislike, blind stereotypical approach, and extremely arrogant and rejecting outlook. This type of prejudice oftentimes stand on selective recognition of one person within a specific ethnic group. This is the type of selective recognition meant to pacify rather than celebrate achievement. Once the selective recognition itself is awarded, it usually remains unchanged for many years. While hundreds or perhaps thousands of people from other ethnic group are enjoying merit-based recognition on an ongoing basis, the person accorded selective recognition within an ethnic group designated to be appeased usually remains the only person for years. How dare the people who are like him or her to complain!

Concealed hate without deep-seated anger is like a bomb built with no way to detonate. Deep-seated anger is the driving force behind concealed hate. This type of anger can be triggered by jealousy, insecurity, natural ability of their target, and their target's determination to excel. Part of the goal of concealed hate is to stop or at a minimum discourage effort, derail aspiration, destroy dreams, and possibly slow down everything necessary to help their target's ambition and the possibility of inspiring anyone within that ethnic group and beyond. If all else fails, deep-seated anger of a person or group of people with concealed hate can reemerge and transform into gratuitous hate. If you believe that a person with concealed hate will eventually repent and have a change of heart, you could be jumping into a lake infested with crocodiles capable of lying low beneath the lake while waiting for the chance to attack and kill. The Bible says, "Be sober, be vigilant; because your adversary the devil, as a roaring lion, walketh about, seeking whom he may devour."

GRATUITOUS HATE

At times our heart ache for logical reason—a way to explain irrational; average person is left with no choice but scratching heads in the effort to make sense or justify the unthinkable, with mouth oftentimes held agape, and sense of reason freezes. Why do people sometimes act irrationally? Why do some people think the best way to settle differences is through "irrational attitude of hostility"? According to the Talmud, this form of hate is the most vicious. It is, for the most part, hinged on the false sense of "right," and the perpetrators believes they must act and fast "we just cannot stand idly by and allow this to continue."

Gratuitous hate, for the most part, can grow out of the desire to purge, to rid the world of transgression, or to eliminate threat or whatever they considered as preventing their selfish and narrow-minded progress. Gratuitous hate can sometimes grow out of irrational sense of "This is ours," or "We are being invaded," or "They are taking over," or "This is demoralizing behavior and we've got to do something about it." This type of hate is vicious with no justification for its inexplicable cruelty and its insidious act of man's inhumanity to man—this is simply evil.

Gratuitous hate is capable of harnessing fear, cultivate apathy and extreme indifference through the spreading of intimidation. It is also capable of turning people against each other and make them act in the defense of the unreasonable agenda or platform that lead to gratuitous hate and openly talk like they too are in on this ungodly mission.

The person or group of people consumed with gratuitous hate passionately believes in their mission and willing to defend it till the end. It does not matter even if God Himself appears to them; their hearts are usually hardened. Gratuitous hate can take on different appearances.

FACES OF HATE

Concealed hate is dangerous and gratuitous hate is malicious. Both are evil and capable of showing up in every facet of human interaction. Either of the two can quickly fill the heart and mind of vulnerable souls irrespective of who they are and irrespective of educational achievement or any significant achievement including status in life. Once unsuspected soul is engulfed, maximum damage in the hand of that captured soul is guaranteed.

Although hate by itself is a powerful and deadly emotion capable of delivering maximum damage, but hate without anger necessary to get it fired up is ineffectual. Anger is the power necessary to propel hate. You need anger to fire up the engine of hate, but you do not need hate to fire up anger. Anger is a necessary emotion that you cannot and should not try to get rid of. You need anger to survive in life, but you do not need hate to survive. No treatment by any health-care professional is designed to cure or eliminate anger but manage it because of its usefulness.

When hate energized by anger is activated the wrong way, it can lead to numb, cold, and calculated reaction completely deaf to the voice of reason, totally bare and alone in its conviction. Anger is capable of blinding the vision of the person inspired by it. Hate can be inadvertently excused and explained away due to the fact that it usually comes in different color and degree. A lot of people have seen hate but fail to recognize it because of human ingenuity, conniving and, at times, subtle and deceiving way of packaging hate.

RAGE-INDUCED HATE

This is spontaneous combustive and highly vicious hate that most people can quickly dismiss as "I lost it" moment. This is by far the most difficult to predict. In most instances, premeditation is often difficult to prove. It is a quiet and silent invader that can engulf and at the same time capable of delivering deadly reaction. This type of hate is in every person everywhere, lying in ambush for the chance to explode. It can exist between husband and wife, between friends, between relatives, and even between a person in position of authority and his or her subjects or subordinates.

Anything can trigger it—tasteless jokes, innocent rejection, interruption perceived as insulting or demeaning, and even prolonged laughter with no chance to explain what the laughter was all about.

It usually sneaks in and engulfs without warning. Part of the underlying reasons are usually due to unresolved emotional issues with diagnosis usually requiring "anger management" as either primary or part of its treatment options. It is capable of unspeakable destructions with no time to think realistically or process consequences logically. It can suddenly come while in transit, hence road rage, or in an event such as sports events or relaxing and entertaining event such as enjoying yourself in the movie theater or recreational event such as deserving time at the amusement park. It can explode even within loving and caring relationship.

Rage, in a person suffering from unresolved emotional issues, or undiagnosed mental health problem can sometime ignore core professional training requirements by using unsubstantiated and irrational excuses such, "I was afraid for my life" even when there was no credible threat. In reality, threat may or may not be present in the situation, but unjustified and perceived threat remains the culprit or the reason for life-threatening and deadly reaction. Rage can leave highly intelligent and God-fearing people scratching their heads while trying to make sense of something completely senseless.

FEAR- OR JEALOUSY-INDUCED HATE

This is usually about something not clear to anyone but the person with this type of (what can be perceived as) unfounded fear or jealousy. It can grow out of a sense of entitlement. Unlike rage-induced hate, it is not sudden but preplanned. It can be activated by perceived but unreal threat. Success or self-improvement or advancement of a rival can lead to fear- and jealousy-induced hate.

There is usually ample time to process consequences; however, consequential reasoning can be ignored, the rule of law (constitutional law, or divine law) can be ignored or justified. Unfounded excuses such as "He was becoming too big and too threatening" can trigger it.

On another level, fear of unfounded competition can activate this type of hate. "I was afraid he might take the only person I ever loved genuinely and sincerely," or "They might take my job and leave me with nothing to live for and possibly left me desolate." Any of these could be the contributing factor or stimuli and perhaps the only reasons and a way to justify reaction that most people might see as stupid.

Underneath fear- or jealousy-induced hate is a person who is genuinely insecure. A person who has developed a false sense of vulnerability! When the threat is exposed, it usually leads to shock and awl reaction such as "I can't believe that this total shenanigan is built on unfounded fear and jealousy. This is really stupid and dumb."

SUBSTANCE-INDUCED HATE

This is hate built on mind-altering agent. When struggling with conscience, substance-induced hate usually seem justified. This type of hate is highly intrusive with intrusive thought difficult to get rid of unless something is done. It is usually likely to rely, for the most part, on unfounded and superficial instinct. When it comes to execution, evidence of premeditation is always present. Method employed could make the execution itself look like a product of disturbed mind and the person behind the execution look paranoid with schizoaffective outlook. It is highly difficult to disregard steps taken prior to the application of substance. Inability to free you from substance-induced hate is what makes it attractive and perhaps thought excusable. Why would anyone go this far to carry out something totally heinous and grotesque?

Substance-induced hate can usually lead to unexpected but highly charged and combustible reaction not shy of becoming deadly. It is easy to blame their extreme reacting attitude and inability to control themselves on the influence of foreign agent such as drugs or alcohol.

To avoid intrusive and ever-present sense of guilt and attention to the rule of law, it is oftentimes more appropriate to allow substance use to temporarily invade the mind rather than permanently deal with the underlying reason for hate.

This type of gratuitous hate often hinges on what people cannot change but prefer to eliminate. If substance influence fails or falls short, this type of hate can quickly shift to concealed hate and difficult to let go until something satisfactory is done.

PRIDE-INDUCED HATE

At times what appears like a legitimate right is actually an abuse of privilege. It is not unheard of to see some people come out with excessive display of baseless pride. Such as: "I sacrificed a lot for this country and now they are giving it to all these undeserving minorities!"

The person with this kind of pride forgets to be grateful for such opportunities available exclusively to him and those within his ethnic group, thereby making him highly successful. When thousands of minorities were denied the right to opportunities—education, employment, financial support including moral support—the same minorities they now see as undeserving could not openly apply for college admission on merit. Many of them had to be ushered into college by Federal troops and stayed in class under the watchful eyes of the same Federal troops. The same minorities had to be protected in the campus, every day, from needless attack.

Those who managed to complete college did not have the privilege to graduate into inestimable opportunities in professional life. They were not privileged to the same pride that comes with college education, independence, the chance to grow, the chance to positively affect the lives of those in their own communities, and the right to live anywhere they so desire. Even with their college education, jobs for minorities were considered rare commodity. Those who were able to find one had to consider themselves lucky for whatever meager job they get. Many could not afford dependable automobiles or a house in the so-called gated communities. Many were cramped in ghettos and el barrios. Depressing songs of poverty became part of the social norms! While members of other ethnic groups were enjoying life to the fullest, the same minorities they so despised were forced to grapple with leftovers.

If you are a minority, you could not walk around with your head held up. Every reference to your existence is punctuated with demeaning and degrading phrases such as "since slavery." If you are intelligent enough to innovate, some smart mouth is going to come from nowhere with smart remark such as "This is one of the skills brought to this country from Africa by slaves." How many other ethnic groups do you know are subject to this type of horrific and insensitive references?

These pride-induced haters had forgotten that along with the ocean of opportunities available to them is the right to set the rules and regulations in college admission, financial institutions, media, in law enforcement, even in government (just to name a few) by which the same minorities are expected to live their lives. The never-ending sense of superiority and endless control continues uninterrupted.

The same minorities were forced to sit in the back of the bus bought by their money as taxpayers. They were denied the right to rest comfortably in hotels and motels including the pride of home ownership. The general conscientious is that minorities just want handouts. "It is a cruel jest to say to a bootless man he ought to lift himself by his own bootstraps." This is 2017, and unfortunately, most of these problems still exist but had gone underground. Concealed hate is still very much alive.

Another aspect of pride-induced hate is refusing to accept other people or refusing to coexist. Statements such as "They are beneath me. I am too good to be associated with these people or possibly connect as members of the same human race" is one of the sustaining powers of discrimination and division.

The people obsessed with pride-induced hate are, needless to say, irrationally arrogant, morally deficient, and not afraid to exercise false claim and pompous attitude to support or justify their baseless pride and ungratefulness. Pride-induced hate is always built on false expectations devoid of a rightly due sense of gratitude. They had forgotten that "to him whom much is given, much is required."

The possibility of pride leading to endless baseless anger and ultimately hate cannot be underestimated. This type of hate can cloud judgment, destroy any iota of godliness remaining, and erode whatever loving attribute is left. It can lead to an ungodly alliance with evil. It can push upright, God-fearing citizens to passionately and secretly support hate group, thereby take on a different, irrational, and extremely vitriolic outlook without regard to the rule of law and without paying attention to the divine call of God. "How dare you compare a man of my integrity, stature, position, and achievement as belonging to the same class and the same human family or human race as these people?"

ABUSE-INDUCED HATE

This is a difficult to forgive and forget betrayal of trust. Many of us are not afraid to love until you are given a reason not to . . . In some cases, it may be easy to forgive because forgiveness is demanded by God. However, it does not always mean you forget—that is humanly impossible to do. The hurt and the disappointment associated with abuse can go on for a lengthy period. Once this type of hate is activated, it is extremely difficult to get rid of.

It can be activated by an unspeakable sense of betrayal or stolen innocence. How do you love after being violated, after being stepped on and trashed, after being treated like a disposable piece of crap!

Abuse-induced hate can lead to constant reminder of a memory you would have loved to suppressed for life. It can wake up to what is known in the medical environment as anxiety or even lead posttraumatic stress disorder (PTSD). It can rob anyone of a lasting sense of security, steal joy, and wake up sense of fear, jittery, and hopelessness. Abuse-induced hate can oftentimes demand retaliation even when retaliatory reaction looks like overreaction. In this case, the ensuing action of the victim can lead to irrational reaction built on simply the desire to do something. "I am not going to let you go scot-free."

Cruel or violent treatment, although evil, has been passively allowed in our society for such a long time. To think that another human being is nothing but a piece of property to be kept or dispose of at will is more than cruel and violent treatment; it is outright evil and ungodly. No one deserves to be abused—not in any way, shape, or form and not for any reason.

Abuse-induced hate can turn children against parents, wife against husband, boyfriend against girlfriend, friends against friends, employees against employers, politicians against constituent. It is capable of driving a wedge or creating a lasting wound and of setting off powerful and destructive bomb.

GREED-INDUCED HATE

This is all about covetousness—a never-ending insatiable desire for more. If not curtailed, it can drive or push anyone to steal, and "if a man would steal, he would kill. If a man would kill, he would destroy." Once activated, it is completely devoid of conscientious awareness and can quickly destroy the voice of reason.

In business, politics, government, and even religion, it is not uncommon to be consumed with greed to the exclusive neglect of original mission or goal. Greed usually starts with an unusual love of something such as money, influence, or power, hence the saying "Absolute power corrupts absolutely."

Another side of greed-induced hate is when an object appears as hinges on one's success or something so dear and worth dying for. Drug dealers, inspired by greed and the desire for territorial control, can turn on each other or become a monster in other to protect an area that they perceived as their territory.

Self-love is one thing. The desire to be consumed with self-interest, as well as going after what is beneficial to you alone to the exclusively neglect of concerns for the well-being of others, is another. When the two are mixed, blind approach to the problems of others becomes the norm rather than the exemption. People could be dying of starvation or lack of adequate health care; greed believes in overwhelming concentration on "What is in this for me?" as opposed to "What can I do to make life worth living for all of God's children??" If this type of desire and self-love is becoming too obvious, they usually devise a means to hide their interest and pretend like there is nothing diabolical in what they do.

In the book of 1 Timothy 6:10, the Bible tells us that "the love of money is the root of all evil: which while some coveted after, they have erred from the faith, and pierced themselves through with many sorrows."

SECRECY-INDUCED HATE

Another potent and highly destructive form of hate is secrecy-induced hate! This is a lying-in-wait hate that is highly disregarding in the sense that the assigned weight of the information you are entrusted with is usually bigger and more important than the trustee. It simply does not matter who you think you are, you've got to protect the secret you are entrusted with and guard it with your life. Otherwise, what you think is your life can end abruptly and unfavorably.

This is, by and large, usually between two individuals, or in rare cases involving small group. Protecting what is expected to be extraordinarily confidential information is not always as easy as it sounds. A lot of people would do anything to keep whatever they considered as secret from falling into the wrong hands. Revealing what is not supposed to be revealed can sometimes end in instantaneous and irrational act of hostility not related to anything else but abuse of trust. It is a time bomb waiting to explode

Some people have the habit to constantly ask for loyalty with reassuring response similar to "Your secret is safe with me." This kind of obsession are oftentimes difficult to explain, most especially when the person expecting reassuring response is highly insecure, unusually suspicious, and very weak when it comes to trusting. Secrecy-induced hate can be avoided if it is possible to let your friends and acquaintances know that coming together as friends or acquaintance will not involve sharing of secret. "I am simply not interested in any information classified as secret."

REVENGE-INDUCED HATE

This is usually concealed hate at its best. Once the mind is set on revenge, forgiveness is not always part of the equation but satisfaction. Expected satisfaction is in knowing that "whoever did this horrific act pays dearly" for whatever the offense. This is so important that God himself had to specifically address it in His word, asking whoever is wronged to leave the revenge to Him. "Vengeance is mine, says the Lord, I will avenge."

Unexpected, undeserving, and sometimes violence unjustified act is always the culprit. When innocence is taken in any way or someone feels violated beyond measure or abused and the desire for revenge is concluded as the only plausible thing to do, nothing satisfies. The perpetrator is marked, and the hope to break even now becomes the goal. It does not matter how important, rich, popular, or strong the perpetrator is. Revenge does not care about what most people might consider important.

LABELS-INDUCED HATE

Last but not the least is label-induced hate. Labels such as *Negro*, or its American version *Nigger*, has since transformed by hate group into a disparaging way of identifying people. It is one of the most provoking and insulting word ever. Labels of this nature can start an unprecedented major conflict. At a minimum, it can lead to an internalized deadly feeling capable of requiring further processing before reacting. The person on the receiving end might say without drawing any conclusion that "you seriously hurt my feelings," and walk away only to act later or show resentment right away.

Why is the label such as "son of a former slave" necessary in this day and age? More importantly, why is it always used exclusively in reference to black people? Every time an African American takes a quantum leap forward and achieve something great, the media usually refer to him as a "son of former slave." Why is this necessary? If they cannot or will not say the same about any Irish person or any other ethnic group with the shameful history of slavery, why do they think it is okay to describe any African American this way? Is this the television network or any branch of the media's way of saying we are not done with the blemish, discrimination, segregation, and prejudice perpetrated on African Americans? Why do they think it is okay to negate the contributions of those Africans who came here as explorer or simply as other members of the human race in search of a way to expand and grow and did not come as a result of slave trade?

Better yet, why do they intentionally disregard and disrespect those African Americans slave owners from other ethnic groups that are not black or connected to Africa? In the eyes of the media, a delicious cousin in New Orleans or elsewhere in the United States is probably the inventor of a slave. Why this assumption with no basis in fact? What if that invention was one of the many originated from African slave owners?

Confederacy dragged a great deal of African Americans who were never slaves but slave owners (of white slaves) into slavery, and the media is still helping the confederacy to preserve the tarnished legacy, shameful history, and reproachful image of slavery pushed on African Americans. Why do they think it is necessary for us to see the future in the ugly mirror of the past that was not truthfully and respectfully told? Are they unaware of the fact that our children need uplifting history that can energize them to want to compete proudly and excel in life?

Label is usually meant to sort and divide "us from them" rather than create inclusiveness. It, no doubt, has an undeniable negative connotation that can demean and anger people to no end, thereby lead to, at a maximum, unprecedented level of deadly conflict. It can lead to a deep gulf of hatred and a never-ending stream of deadly confrontation.

As revealed by Dr. Kwame Nantambu, "*Negro* is an adjective which means black in Portuguese and Spanish." But since the beginning of the slave trade, the adjective *Negro* became a noun and the legitimate name of a newly enslaved people" (emphasis mine). The world emphasized here is done to show you that black people were not the first to fall into the dehumanizing slave trade. What happened to the other ethnic group (white) brought to the United States as slaves? Those Africans sold into slavery and ended up in the hand of the Portuguese and eventually the Spanish were few in numbers, but black people unfortunately became the poster child of slave trade. As part of this shameful turn of event is the label that was supposed to be innocent translation of language quickly changed to a derogatory and dehumanizing way to refer to an entire ethnic group.

What about the subtle and nonthreatening labels such "African American," "Irish American," "German American," even "black" or "white"! Why are all these necessary? Why is it necessary to label highly qualified CEO of a reputable company "black CEO" and not just "CEO"? When would the media realize that they are not helping but further dividing? If the media is doing it to show that the board of director of whatever company is in compliance with affirmative action, it is, needless to say, very divisive and highly unnecessary. Affirmative action will not be necessary if not for the way we have turned against one another. Africans or African Americans would like to compete and earn their rightful place purely based on merit.

Discrimination is embedded and inscribed in labels. Labels provide a way to discriminate rather than unite people. It makes it possible to push provoking thought, actions, and reactions without realizing that this is discriminatory. It makes it possible for agents of hate to quickly activate hate and discrimination before examining the fact and before the object of this incendiary label even had a chance. Regulatory encouraged declaration such as "I am white," "I am black," "I am African American," or "I am Irish American" or "I am Asian American" just to name a few are highly unnecessary, divisive, and too segregating. There is nothing wrong with simply saying: "I am an American" or "I am a US citizen." After all, we are all citizens of the only country whose constitution begins with the phrase "We the People."

Another label often used as a weapon of separation is usually hidden in the desire to know what exactly is going on. Example, if you heard that one of your children is in love and just met a potential significant other, the desire to want to know about his or her ethnicity could be based on more than just innocent desire to know. If one of the questions asked is "Who is this person?" You do not need the wisdom of Solomon to know that the person asking the question could be probing deeper or perhaps fishing for a way to approve or disapprove with the choice already made rather than looking for information. Most people in love would have loved to volunteer an explicit response such as "That's none of your business." However, the desire for validation may prompt some to reluctantly provide what they would have loved to keep to themselves.

What does it matter whether the person your child is in love with is white, black, Asian, or Hispanic? This kind of intrusive effort to know could lead to uninvited objection and reactivation of a long-suppressed concealed hate.

I mentioned in volume 1 of *Culprit of Division* how God never referred to any of His children by outward appearance but by lineage and genealogy. Isn't it amazing that Christ never deviated from the same! Nowadays, people are curious and exceedingly itching to know more about those mentioned in the Bible, most especially how they look on the outside and what part of the world they came from or call home.

Why is it necessary to see your fellow members of the human family different from how God sees them? The label such as "people of color" carries a negative connotation and unjustified assumption that there is a prevailing and acceptable skin color. Why is it necessary to still continue to use this divisive label: "people of color"? Why is it necessary to establish derogatory label not uplifting by any measure? Why is it necessary to dehumanize others just to make yourself and those like you look better with false sense of superiority? Why is it necessary to enact laws that limit interactions, infringe on freedom, and force people to feel guilty about falling in love, which was not included in divine law or not expected to be legislated in any way by any government under the heaven?

As revealed in *Virginia Encyclopedia* by Brendan Wolfe,

> Racial integrity laws passed by the General Assembly to protect "whiteness" against what many Virginians perceived to be the negative effects of race-mixing. They included the Racial Integrity Act of 1924, which prohibited interracial marriage and defined as white a person any individual "who has no trace whatsoever of any blood other than Caucasian" like as if to say that Caucasians are not part of the human family. The same law also required all public meeting spaces to be strictly segregated; and a third act, passed in 1930, that defined as black a person who has even a trace of African ancestry. This way of defining whiteness as a kind of purity in bloodline became known as the "one drop rule." These laws arrived at a time when a pseudo-science of white superiority called eugenics gained support of groups like the Anglo-Saxon Clubs of America. Part of their arguments include that the mixing of whites, African Americans, and Virginia Indians could cause great societal harm, really? What about those among them whose bloodline can be traced to Africa? They are, no doubt, Africans
>
> Virginia Indians were particularly incensed by the laws and by Plecker in particular, because the state seemed intent bent on removing any legal recognition of Indian identity in favor of the broader category "colored." After one failed try, lawmakers largely achieved this goal in 1930, drawing negative reaction from the black press. The Racial

Integrity Act remained on the books until 1967, when the U.S. Supreme Court, in *Loving v. Virginia*, found its prohibition of interracial marriage to be unconstitutional. In 2001, the General Assembly denounced the act, and eugenics, as racist.

The people behind this prejudicial, discriminating, and segregating law refused to recognize the presence of God in the kingdom of men. They refused to accept the fact about the only one race "the human race." They came up with a law clearly meant to sort, segregate and divide all of us into categories not divinely sanctioned.

There were many attempts in the past such as legislative attempts, institutional attempts, and even individual attempts. However, kings, queens, and their kingdoms got hold of some of the divisive words that have been affecting our society, and they refused to let go. Some of these words made it through laws, ordinances, and even companies' policies and procedures. Hate group took them and many of the hateful studies done to a different level, but all to no avail. There is simply no place for all these deplorable words or labels in any discussions, jokes, or in any civilized society and most especially no place for it among black people either.

What difference would it make if one of your children is in love with someone of another ethnic group? The beauty of love is divine. What difference would it make if the person who steps forward to donate the vital organ you need to survive is of another ethnic group? What difference would it make if the killer of a loved one is from a different ethnic group? Would it make any difference to know that the employer is of a different ethnicity?

If you are concerned about society or those in your inner circle and what they think or might think, you are merely serving self to the exclusive neglect of what God thinks. The fact that our minds, eyes, choices, and preferences have been invaded, highjacked, and rewired cannot be ignored. Our world is under the influence of hate.

HATE IN RELIGION

Nothing can be more complicated! Religion is expected to exist for the benefit of the human family—a way to worship God and remain connected to Him. However, the presence of mortal in the affairs of immortal is bound to invite something unholy and unacceptable but permissible because of what is ordained and given to us—freedom to choose. Our free volition gives us the freedom to accept or reject the plan of God. If you think God is going to rain fire from heaven every time we misbehave, you simply do not understand God, His attributes, and His nature.

Organizers of religion can deviate from the original goal and purpose of religion, thereby taking on what is known as concealed anthropomorphic appearance. It may be completely different from what God would have loved to see, but His mercy will not allow Him to abandon those He created in His own image. Some of the people behind religion may have transformed themselves into an anthropomorphic being in human outlook along with attributes, no doubt incarnate of the same, but God remains "the same, yesterday, today, and forever."

Anthropomorphic is defined as a "nonhuman 'being' with human form or human attributes. They

Drawing provided by Ronya Balogun - Author's wife

have the appearance and behavior of human beings, but their animal-like characteristics" and attributes cannot be ignored. If the almighty God is who they think He is or who they perceived Him to be, the world would be in great danger. They think like, act like, judge like, or at a minimum behave like human beings; but in reality, their behavior proves otherwise. Shedding of human blood or the destruction of human life pleases them beyond measure. Inflicting suffering and pain confirms their narrow understanding of God. Their god is merciless and delights in the suffering of people. To them, human beings are no better than a disposable man-made product. The most astounding and bewildering fact about them is that they cannot exist without the same human beings they are out to get and destroy.

If God sees the people He created in His own image the way these misinformed religious group sees them, you might as well forget about a separate being known as the devil. God and the devil would, no doubt, be one and the same. It's good to know that we are all precious in the eyes of the merciful God

Not only do these caricatures who like to prove that they are religious and doing the will of God genuinely hate what God created; these self-centered and selfish religious, but in reality the devil incarnate, believe that they are ordained by God to instantly judge and punish those who fail to accept their picture of God and their so-called proper way to worshiping Him. To them, it is okay to kill unbelievers which are generally regarded as infidels—even their own children, blood of the same blood; and people within the same religious sect cannot escape their cruelty and wickedness. Organized religion exists to guide people to God, but their religion exists to separate and isolate God from the people He created in His own image. To them, hate is a tool that must be used indiscriminately.

The desire to worship and admire God, thereby hear from Him and feel His presence, is the main reason for coming together in the form of an organized religion. Regardless, people can still reach out to God without the so-called organized religion. In reality, there is nothing divine about the way it is organized or about the way people are forced to worship—somehow, it is edifying, and God encourages it.

However, to have perfectly changed something set up with good intent, something so uplifting, something so presumably godly in the interest of narrow and destructive desire is amazing to say the least. The divine plan of God, which has not been unanimously sanctioned, interpreted, and explained, is not unaware of what is happening in our world, hence the consoling word of Christ to His followers: "Ye shall know the truth and the truth shall set you free."

The main religions of the world such as Christianity, Islam, Judaism, Buddhism, Hinduism, Confucianism, and Taoism, to name just a few, are yet to prove in action that they all exist to worship and love the same God. Their individualized beliefs, tenets, and method make it extremely difficult to think that they are all talking about the same God.

Ordination as a servant of God, which was once believed to be a private one-on-one divine calling and anointing, has been, for the most part, replaced exclusively by training, family influence, or size of donation to a specific denomination or organization. There are some cases where the only requirement could be: life experience or perceived dedication or simply by what Vexen Crabtree described as "shared collections of transcendental beliefs that have been passed on from believers to converts. It is believed by adherents to be actively meaningful and serious and either based on (1) formally documented doctrine (organized religion) or (2) established cultural practices (folk religion)."

The problem is not how you are called. There is nothing wrong with how you hear, respond, and submit yourself to God for service. The only problem with what we have nowadays is that the truth, along with the divine connection, is no longer part of the requirements. Those who take it at face value oftentimes do so at their own peril based on highly convincing testimonies and carefully crafted life of those professing to have been called and how they see and relate to people. Outward display of holiness and the false appearance of exclusive connection to God are not only deceitful but wrong at every level. The Bible says, "Ye shall know them by their fruits."

Unsuspecting believers/followers are usually the one to do whatever dirty work needed and necessary to keep some of these religions alive, even if the religion and its mission are so dangerous, completely antihuman, and diametrically opposed to the will of God.

FAILURE OF RELIGION

The current mission and purpose of some religion are currently unclear—many of them are gradually deviating and shifting into something highly secular, more subjective and wickedly stealth-like approach deeply rooted and grounded in concealed hate. Needless to say, religion has become too self-serving, imposing, and methodically and diabolically discriminating. As much as many would have loved to see religion involve in and embark on loving humanity, the opposite, unfortunately, has become the new norm.

Religion has shifted from theocracy to aristocratic rule with something that looked godly but wickedly hateful, divisive, discriminating, and, no doubt, prejudicial with holier-than-thou attitude in much respect. Peaceful coexistence, although not openly resented, but by the same token, not openly and genuinely approved and embraced either. In a way, religion has become the undisputable home of concealed hate, carefully crafted prejudice, and no doubt the breeding ground for gratuitous hate.

Religion is currently the most toxic organization and clearly the most recognized platform of hate all around the world. Many people have lost their lives in religious-inspired hate than any other conflict in the history of human existence.

One religion believes that those who are called and ordained are expected to go out and convince the rest of the human family through preaching and never-ending display of a life full of samples. The core of their message is "Whosoever will, let him come." Another religion believes that you have to come to them even if they have never done anything to convince you or give you a reason why you should come to them. If you fail to come, they have no choice but to force you or even kill you if you resist. To say that they take comfort in the number of people they are able to eliminate is an understatement. On the other hand, some other religion believes in passive approach—if you come to us, great, and if you refused to come, that's equally great as well.

There are some other religions so localized, ethnic-oriented or mainly for a specific country to the exclusive neglect of others. Their goal is not to save the world, and their preaching are not for any other people outside of their domain (country of origin) and couldn't care less if the world is facing annihilation or not. Their modus operandi is "live and let's live." Their theology openly rejects preventive action or preemptive reaction even when their existence is threatened and extinction of their existence is imminent. They are not necessarily advocating nonviolence but nonresistance. Their passive reaction is openly practiced.

Their members are not too big on forgiving those who offended them in any way, shape, or form. Inability to forgive others of offense, even minor offense, can go on forever. Messagewise, the foundation of their faith is complicated and membership is not well informed as to the best approach or how to handle conflict. Most of what you can refer to in the Bible are interpreted differently, and explanation provided by leadership is more revered, separating and isolating than unifying, edifying, uplifting, and completely devoid of glorifying God.

In this day and age of shifting position and of misrepresentation within a religion with regard to divine calling and anointing, no one can be accused of being skeptical or being leery in exercising blind faith. Many people are jumping on the bandwagon of service without any divine connection necessary to be effective. Moses heard the voice of God, and the same with Samuel and Jeremiah to name a few! Elijah, David, and many like them were chosen and preordained! Joshua, Elisha, and many others learned from their masters, thereby receiving the right to serve! Isaiah heard that God was looking for whom to send, and Isaiah stepped forward and said, "Here I am, Lord, send me." No matter how you looked at it, the calling of any of those was not without divine stamp of approval.

Jesus personally called His disciples, trained and prepared them for service. Later, in the upper room, He increased the number of those disciples and commissioned them including Paul, who He called on the way to Damascus to "go out and preach the Gospel." They were fully ready for the fulfillment of their higher calling. Jesus said, "No man can come to me except the Father draws him." The calling of those disciples, undoubtedly divine, was meant to continue where Jesus left off.

Human hand and involvement in something so personal and requiring ongoing connection to Him who still "rules in the affairs of men" is without a doubt lacking authenticity and clarity of what the calling is all about. The voice of the board of directors had replaced the voice of God. Controlling how far a servant of God can go in the obedience of his calling is, needless to say, in the hand of rich and influential members of the church. Uninhibited interaction is completely out. Sinners can no longer come in—they are simply too distracting, and their actions too tempting. A servant of God of a different ethnic group cannot officiate as the senior pastor of a denomination different from his or her ethnicity even though they are not unaware of the fact that we are all members of the same human family. They are not unaware of the need for peaceful coexistence ordained by God and its importance in the church of God.

Theocracy is out and aristocracy is in. To say that we are living in the age of extraordinary intrusion and human control built on self-serving attitudes and concealed negative behaviors of the rich and influential to the exclusive neglect of what God wants is an understatement. Many of these organizations are not concerned about "what would Jesus do." They are not designed to serve humanity but further divide them.

When the church of God is highjacked, and the only link between man and God (the servant of God) is relegated to the level of a favored employee that can be controlled as opposed to a revered and highly respected indispensable representative of the Most High, the church becomes the breeding ground for concealed hate and, eventually, gratuitous hate. When the man of God is no longer the man of God, politics and secular teachings creep in—morality, the truth, and the power of prayer takes the backseat. The church then become almost like a club of like-minded people but still retains the appearance of the house of God. We are left with only one choice, and that is the effort to try and understand God.

EXTREMISTS AND HATE

Dr. Martin Luther King Jr once said that "hate is too great a burden to bear." Hate is a destroyer with no conscience. No one can become extremist without the foundation required to make impact. They have to hate something, people or social program. Maximum impact is usually their goal without remorse and without repentance. Being a revolutionist cuts across the gamut of human interaction. However, being a radical and extremist places one on a different level. In most cases, being a radicals or extremist means you have taken an unyielding position that has led you to desire change and hate whatever opposes your view passionately. The hate that comes with your new platform can be toxic if it is done to the exclusive neglect of appreciation and love necessary to connect you, emotionally or otherwise, to the human family.

To harbor hate is to harbor evil. It can transform any well-meaning human being into a monster completely stripped of human traits and attributes. It is not impossible for anyone with deep raw passion not rooted in God's love to antagonize whatever they see as standing in the way of their mission, even if it is demanding losing human lives in the end. It is not equally impossible to not make every effort to block opposing views on whatever they perceived as worth dying for. They have to go through period of transformation whereby they are changed into something equal to anthropomorphic being while struggling to maintain what look and appear like "human attributes, traits, emotions, and intentions."

Extremists are not always unaware of the fact that their efforts, no doubt toxic, can be seen as clearly and completely anticivility and antipeaceful coexistence. To try to turn back willingly without divine intervention is impossible. Their minds are usually programmed and hardened.

They are capable of rewiring their own system to not listen to the voice of conscience and reason, to not process anything that tends to oppose their position on whatever it is they considered dear to them. Their knowledge and whatever remaining in them are there to defend and support their agenda even if unpopular, extremely painful, unacceptable, and constitute acts of man's inhumanity to man. They are simply blinded to everything else and not afraid to shut anybody out including God.

It is not impossible for them to become suspicious of anyone even those within their immediate family. By the time they realize their self-created isolation, pessimistic attitude, and better-than-anyone persona, paranoia has taken over, and everything about them from this point forward is going to encourage more isolation. This is when constructive criticism gets more irritating and pushes them farther away from people.

Extremists tend to operate within religion (any religion), within politics or government. They are usually arrogant and not afraid to declare themselves as highly intelligent, better-than-average person, and above reproach and blemish. A person with extremist tendency tends to draw strength from past or current extremists—they are undoubtedly his heroes and admirers. If they are in politics or government, they usually draw strength from other extremist in politics or in government. The same goes for extremists in religion. Extremists simply do not believe in correction necessary to please anyone including God. They are not for establishing better relationship with anyone. It is often difficult for them to apologize for mistakes made even if it was unintentional.

On the other hand, some extremists, most especially in religion, are lucky to find a loving, plausible, and godly way out before it becomes too late and before their mission becomes too deadly. In the book of Acts chapter 9 (NIV) is the story of a man named Saul of Tarsus. Saul was a very religious man who genuinely believes in obedience to the rule of law. However, Saul was a lightweight extremist with a murderous tendency, intent, and undeniable "threats against the Lord's disciples." Obedience to the rule of law (usually absent from hard-core extremists) was what made him a lightweight extremist. The same obedience to the rule of law prompted him to go to the high priest with one—and only one—request. He went to the high priest to ask him "for a letter to the synagogues in Damascus, so that if he found any there who belonged to the Way, whether men or women, he might take them as prisoners to Jerusalem." If they resist, Saul could have, at a minimum, injured them or at a maximum kill them. However, "as he neared Damascus on his journey, suddenly a light from heaven flashed around him. He fell to the ground and heard a voice say to him, 'Saul, Saul, why do you persecute me?'" Although Saul was not the only one who heard the voice, but the message was unmistakably meant for him and him only.

Saul realized that this was bigger than him—something not very common to extremists. No one can be perceived to be bigger than a typical hard-core extremist. Saul asked "Who are you, Lord?" To acknowledge that this must be the Lord talking to him speaks volume. The voice said, "'I am Jesus, whom you are persecuting, I want you to get up and go into the city, and you will be told what you must do.'

"The men traveling with Saul stood there speechless and motionless; they heard the sound but did not see anyone. Saul got up from the ground, but when he opened his eyes he could not see anything. So they led him by the hand into Damascus. For three days he was blind and did not eat or drink anything." He was, no doubt, going through a period of preparation and transformation designed by the Lord to mold him into the person God wanted him to be.

To cut a long story short, "in Damascus there was a disciple named Ananias. The Lord called to him in a vision, 'Ananias!' 'Yes, Lord,' Ananias answered. The Lord told him, 'Go to the house of Judas on Straight Street and ask for a man from Tarsus named Saul, for he is praying. In a vision he (Saul) has seen a man named Ananias come and place his hands on him to restore his sight.'"

Ananias was not unaware of who he was asked to meet, hence the response "Lord, I have heard many reports about this man and all the harm he has done to your holy people in Jerusalem. And he has come here with authority from the chief priests to arrest all who call on your name." But the Lord said to Ananias, "Go! This man is my chosen instrument to proclaim my name to the Gentiles and their kings and to the people of Israel. I will show him how much he must suffer for my name." In the end, Saul was transformed into Paul, an apostle and a follower of Christ.

If Saul was a hard-core extremist, he could have defied the voice. He could have said something similar to the following: "You think you can fool me into believing the voice of someone invisible? I don't think so." When he was knocked down and unable to see, he could have said something to the effect of "You think blinding my eyes will force me to abandon my mission? Think again." Saul did not resist. He did not see himself above reproach or higher than the almighty. The desire to obey the Lord was in him all along. He was simply not a hard-core extremist.

When Abraham Lincoln, the president of the United States, took the step necessary to unite the nation and create genuine equality, the hard-core extremist formed their own government otherwise known as Confederacy. They became rebellious beyond measure. Their goal was to control and demoralize an important part of the population. They rose up against those who simply wanted their own rightful place in the land they worked so hard for. These were hardworking citizens who were not interested in handouts. They were proud and dignified people. The confederate soldiers refused to let them enjoy peaceful coexistence. They refused to listen to the government, and they refused to listen to God almighty. They were bent on destruction never before seen in history. They ganged up against free men and women of African descent and decided to smear them with the blemish of slavery. They had forgotten that the "Most High" still rules in the affairs of men and will eventually have the last say.

Confederate soldiers and their sympathizers remained unyielding and extremely violent. They had forgotten that the effort to force freedom out of black people will one day force them to stand up taller than ever before, thereby prove through determination and resilient attitude "that all men are created equal."

The effort of the Confederate soldiers and their sympathizers along with those false theories and histories including all the discriminating laws before them paved the way for the rising of one of the most gruesome and the most repugnant act ever experienced in the hand of hateful group called KKK. Those who lost their lives as a result of their inexplicable act of man's inhumanity to man did not die in vain.

Hate will, in the end, consume and destroy the one who harbors hate. It does not matter what kind of reward you think God is going to shower you with in heaven or what you think you would get for the killing, the persecution, inflicting pain, and making life difficult for all of God's children! Your place in hell is undeniably certain and guaranteed.

HATE IN POLITICS

The road to peaceful coexistence is seeded with hidden live bombs capable of exploding if not properly and carefully removed and discarded. The desire of many to feel like they are ordained by God to rule and control the world is nothing short of selfish desire that has plagued the human family for years. It is an open door to endless greed and horrendous act of man's inhumanity to man. Politics, one of many places you do not expect hate, is nowadays riddled with the presence of many unrepentant agents of hate who are looking for a way to solidify and imprint their agenda where they believe it should have maximum and lasting impact. Part of their goal is to establish and seal the footprint of hate in human affairs for good and help make the presence of hate permanently hidden in an unsuspected and nonthreatening manner. If it helps put a "would-be dictator" in power, so be it. However, if you are naïve enough to reject and quickly dismiss hate in politics, you may be in for a surprise.

They are there among lawmakers; they are in the midst of those in executive branch as well as the judicial branch. Although they are not easy to detect, but they are there! Running for public office is not necessarily about the intent to help anyone or make life easier for electorates. It usually about what those running for public office believe is missing or what should be embraced. It's about personal philosophy, deep-seated ideology. It's about rearranging things the way they see it or believe how things should be rearranged. Election, in most cases, provides a way to get in and create change. Election or the desire to force their way into government is a stepping stone to total control only available at the citadel of power.

Human intervention in the plan of God is one of the major culprits of division in our world. Politics had paved the way for unspeakable hate ever unleashed by some of the world's most heartless, most wicked. and most evil privileged few as well as the ruthless dictators in human history. They had managed to achieve their objectives though politics.

Selfish desire prompted kings, queens, and their kingdoms to believe that they were ordained to meddle in the affairs of God, thereby deciding on who is qualified to be a legitimate member of the human family including those who are qualified to be called children of God. Some people were treated with dignity and respect while others were scorned, abused, and humiliated beyond imagination. This kind of action gave people within the ethnic group of the self-proclaimed elite, a false sense of superiority and arrogant personality, which led them to the ungodly disparaging rush to assign the label of "dark continent" on the birth place of mankind while other places were regarded as the "city of light," or "the land of hope." They greatly enjoyed exclusive treatment beyond expectation while others were mistreated, vilified, demeaned, suffered tremendous abuse and even death.

They placed themselves so high above the rest and equal to God. They even went as far as created a different set of rules and regulations necessary and required (in their judgment and different from what the Bible says) to become a Christian. They placed too much burden on others and only those in their circle can boldly step forward and truly enjoyed the goodness of the Lord in the land of the living. They were under the impression that their desire to govern, rule, and control the world was presanctioned by God. They even went as far as to think that God was a "chartered member of the white citizen's council." All their actions and reactions paved the way for greater division, which allowed much more wicked people to jump on the bandwagon. Discrimination, segregation, and unspeakable prejudice among the children of God were expected as long as it was sanctioned by the dynasty in charge.

In those days, refusing—or at a minimum, forgetting—to say "God bless the queen" was enough to start war, unimaginable loss of life, and complete isolation from the human family. It was enough to make them relegate a nation and people to the level of subhuman. They refused to believe that "all men are created equal." Facts about indisputable atrocity unleashed on those different from them remain indelible in the hearts and minds of victims all over the world. How can we forget? An English man by the name William Shakespeare (I'm quite sure you remember him) once wrote, "The evil that men do lives after them, the good often interred with their bones."

There was no denying the fact that missionary activities grew tremendously in the Americas in the seventeenth centuries. The same can be said about the rest of the world. However, you couldn't call yourself a Christian or be recognized as such if you fail to meet the standard set by the Queen and the British government. Their involvement in Christianity led to a new standard different from what the Bible says.

The unauthorized meddling of kings, queens, and their kingdom in what they had no jurisdiction over and were neither allowed by God in any way, shape, or form set a new level of hate against humanity. It created a rift and ungodly separation. It brought about a higher form of segregation and discrimination designed to indirectly allow dictators to plant seeds of wickedness never before seen in history. Prior to the declaration by Thomas Jefferson that "all men are created equal," most of the laws enacted with the blessings of the Queen were meant to divide "us from them," providing a false sense of supremacy.

The Church of England's role in the marriage of religion and politics cannot be overlooked. To regulate what was not supposed to be regulated by anyone or any earthly government made England and her monarchy equal to god. They placed themselves above blemish and set in motion the kind of division never advocated anywhere in the scripture and definitely not by Christ.

We now have politics all over the world built on concealed hate and politicians serving on the platform of concealed hate. Contrary to expectations and contrary to their deceiving messages, as well as diplomatic and conniving demeanor, their mission and agenda are not for the welfare of the human family but self-serving, intrusive, controlling, and wicked in many respects.

Politics designed to further punish the poor rather than help and lift them up is ungodly. Politics designed to enrich those within the circle of the ruling party to the exclusive neglect of the general public is ungodly. Politics that fail to acknowledge what is important to God as presented in His word is ungodly. Politics that keep looking for approval from religious group with no intention to listen to the truth as declared by God is ungodly. Act of politician that tends to seek divine approval and blessing to the exclusive neglect of divine message and truth is ungodly.

We now have politicians who will not lose sleep if a great number of his or her constituent go to bed hungry or have no means of attending to life-threatening illness through adequate health-care insurance. It does not matter, even if many are left to grapple with demeaning life style.

Hate is not always easy to detect in politics because of the fact that it can manifest itself under the canopy of law pending or passed, ideology embraced, and how well they appeal to the fear, apathy, and unsubstantiated concerns of their base. Politics makes it possible to be conniving and resentful without showing destructive resentment and to not be so vocal about any concealed disdain and hate for their target, which could be a specific ethnic group, social issues or whatever they so passionately hate.

Politics provide a conducive environment for greed and secrecy-induced hate. Part of their strategies is to be bold, look believable and truthful but, in reality, simply lies all the way to the top through the presentation of unrealistic and vain promises including made-up stories and assumptions. Once they get to the top, things are bound to begin to unfold little by little. The future shock can be drastic, slow-paced, or brutal right from the start—it depends on how solid they perceived their base is. If their base is blindly following them no matter what, the speed at which they unleash can be fast and furious, swift and deadly.

Taking away beneficial social services is usually the beginning followed by unexpected and unsuspected stripping of rights. Oppositions might start to disappear, thereby sending fears and chill to those who might want to say or do something contrary. Unsolicited journalistic view is going to be suppressed faster than you can say the word *fast*. They usually coin and fabricate, and no one is allowed to question their view or sources of their fabrications due to the fact that they are exclusively right. In a way, politics and hate can quickly become a ruthless bedfellow with such an extraordinary and unimaginable transformation. Getting people to defend them or lie for them or follow their every twist and turn with many ways to rationalize their actions is not unexpected and unheard of—birds of the same feather, flock together.

UNFORTUNATE STORY OF THE PAST

We did not see any pictures from the past concerning complete composition of the human family other than the descriptions presented in the scripture and drawn from various subjective imaginations. The outward appearance and characteristics of those before us was a big puzzle left for all of us to put together. Those presented based on imagination are too subjective to be accepted as true. Genealogy provided a clue that is not so clear cut—a clue that anyone with a solid media platform can manipulate and present in any way favorable to them and their ethnicity.

Just like the past, the future is not any clearer. As a result, we have no idea what lies ahead or what the future holds. Paul, the apostle of Christ, tells us that "for now we see through a glass, darkly." He then went on to emphasize that at the appointed time, we shall see "face-to-face." Not only that, the future outward look, including what the skin color of members of the human family would look like, is not known to us also. One of the apostles named John tells us, "Dear friends, now we are children of God, and what we will be has not yet been made known. But we know that when Christ appears, we shall be like him, for we shall see him as he is."

As for the past, we had that Moses, an Israelite, was adopted by a member of Egyptian dynasty—an authentic African dynasty. There was no reference made as to his outward appearance. The fact that he was accepted as a prince of Egypt and in line to become the next king of

Egypt speaks volume. Nothing said about how he looked. Israelites lived many years in Egypt, and there was no reference made as to their outward appearance as well as that of Egyptians. It was never noted that they were different from one another. In the interest of emphasis, Egypt, one of the first cradles of civilization, is in Africa and, again, authentically Africans in many respects.

Egypt was later colonized by the British and, after that, became occupant land of Italian and some other foreign powers. There was no reference prior to all these foreign invasion of Egypt as to their original outward appearance other than what we have seen through archeological discoveries. Archeologists have tried to show us what the past looked like. Their findings remain just a story to be embraced as true and authentic or ignored as too subjective, depending on who is reading it or listening to the story.

One of the most popular among many women of King Solomon was the Queen of Sheba. Besides the fact that the Bible says that she epitomizes beauty, there was no reference as to her outward appearance. We now know through archaeological discoveries that the queen was from Ethiopia, and part of her treasures were found in Ethiopia. In his article entitled "Archaeologists Strike Biblical gold with the discovery of the Queen of Sheba's fabled mines," Damien Gayle wrote, "An ancient gold mine, together with the ruins of a temple, has been found on the high Gheralta plateau in northern Ethiopia, part of the Queen's former territory. The entrance lay concealed behind a 20 ft. stone or slab carved with a sun and crescent moon, the 'calling card of the land of Sheba,' according to excavation leader Louise Schofield."

MIND OF MAN REPROGRAMMED

Hate forced many of us to see the rest of the human family different from how God created and sees them. Instead of continuing with the way it has always been, we came up with labels that were never there. Labels and outward depiction, along color line, of the human family are nothing but the devil's way of separating and dividing people against one another. The devil is not unaware of the kind of hate, segregation, and discrimination likely to come out of this kind of division.

Evil decided to spread its wings among the human race through carefully planned strategies developed and methodically implemented. Africa and some other places became soft target of interest. They knew that any opposition both from within and without can be contained. What was the motivation for this?

AFRICA AND THE DESTRUCTIONS FROM WITHIN

Africa, the land that was exclusively or for the most part regarded as the original garden of Eden, was no doubt sitting on a lot of mind-shattering vast acres and miles of natural resources including gold among many. Africa became the envy of many people and pwers. The desire to take advantage of the land of blessing was too tempting for many to overlook. Not only that, the fact that Africans were unsuspecting, unprepared, and not well organized and equipped to resist invasion and forceful removal of what is rightfully theirs was shown in every action of the opportunists.

Africa was too fragmented and complicated to unite as one. With so many languages, culture, and territorial control, communicating with each other was impossible. There was no shortage of discombobulated dynasties with no formidable or central power, command, and voice. Too many rulers and kingdom that were completely unaware of the value and importance of what they had. Rulers and warriors were seen presenting human offerings and sacrifice to whatever gods. There was little or no regard for human life coupled with an unprecedented nonchalant attitude for the preservation of what is dear, precious, and worth preserving.

If you think that you are a formidable warrior or an important personality to behold, you might soon discover that you can be replaced in a heartbeat. Everything depends on who you are competing with or who your personality intimidates the wrong way, or the kind of notoriety you've earned or trying to earn. If they perceived that you are becoming too popular, too big, too influential, and too dominant, you might find yourself standing alone, facing monumental attack from within and from foreign powers.

What is considered as important is the idea of living in the now—aim for the good things of life without paying attention to lasting and dependable legacy through saving and productive live. Party like there is no tomorrow with out-of-this-world interest in foreign-made goods to the exclusive neglect of all homemade products. It is easy for Africans to walk away from their own people and condemn their effort, know-how, innovative ability likely to increase productivity, employment, and strength. You do not have to travel so far to witness genocide. You can quickly see that no one is indispensable—many Africans does not believe in supporting or patronizing creative minds among them. If neglect and isolation do not discourage or kill him or her, evil attack will. Those who believe that they are ordained with whatever unknown evil power and influence are not afraid to use it on their own people. Deadly jealousy abounds everywhere.

It is not too difficult to see that Africans lack some of the things necessary to defeat aggression and hostility such as the following:

1. One formidable voice
2. Self-love
3. Genuine interest in their own people
4. Support for creativity
5. Growth-driven patronage
6. Organization, and
7. Leadership

The kind of blind love, trust, dependency, and following of everything European is alarming to say the least. Each country in Africa was more susceptible to outside attack and invasion in those days than any other places on earth. Warriors of one tribe couldn't care less about the warrior from another tribe. If anything, they were more interested in the defeat of one another rather than creating a unifying force. They could have formed one kingdom and one power in each country and stay connected to other countries, thereby forming one strong continental power difficult to defeat. Instead, they became separated, less trusting of one another; linguistic issues made it difficult to come together, thereby becoming scattered and weak. Even today, in this day and age, how many African countries are concerned about becoming a force to be reckoned with or a nation deeply interested in those with technological know-how among them or a nation interested in gaining upper hand in military might, or ambitious enough to jump into the development of nuclear energy?

Self-love, self-interest and the desire to protect your land and people are expected to lead to strength as well as strong self-defense. The hope and strength of any nation is in the hand of his population and most especially creative minds and intellectuals among them. A nation desiring to be strong must be willing to tap into what is important such as innovative ambition and patriotism of their citizens including the desire to go out on a limb for your country. Citizens who are, in the words of John F. Kennedy, not concerned about "what their country can do" for them "but what they can do for their country" should be encouraged and supported and not taken for granted or neglected.

Africans are not afraid to doubt the knowledge, creativity, and innovative ambition of their fellow. The desire of Africans is to turn around and embrace everything Europeans. There is simply no desire or inspiration to look within. Although they are upset about the history of the past, but there is nothing done to change it through strong preparation for whatever lies ahead.

The misnomer planted by demeaning studies after studies and erroneous history forced upon them has reprogrammed their minds to believe that black is inferior in every aspect of life. The land that used to provide for the world transformed into the land of starvation and of suffering.

The desire to turn things around should begin with the effort to remove inferiority complex and hate invented and handed over to them. The desire of those agents of hate willing to replace the plan of God cannot be defeated with nonchalant attitude.

THE FUTURE IS NOT A GIFT

We have seen the past, we have seen how things are today, what are we doing to make sure the future is bright

Greed-induced hate got hold of our world and the exploitation with so many layers of discontent and cultural bias set in. Ambition and divisive studies solidified the ungodly aspiration of the so-called privileged few. They became overly intoxicated with the desire to steal, destroy, and kill. They invented a way to justify their overreaching ambition and, as a result, couldn't care less about who was affected. Forget about conscience and divine dictate! They are already numb to those things, and nothing matters but material things in life. Many people and places in Africa were left destitute and completely stripped of what is rightfully theirs.

We cannot avoid not to learn from the past to shape the future. The past is revealed to help some people to step out against hate in favor of positive action necessary to defeat division, greed-induced hate, exploitation, as well as the false sense of supremacy that comes with segregation.

There are so many layers of discontent and cultural bias to sift through. Divisive studies likely to further divide the human family cannot and should not be allowed to rear its ugly head anywhere in the world again.

BURIED HISTORY REVEALED

Many ethnic groups affected by slavery had managed to escape its stigma, shed the blemish of the past, rewrite history to reflect their undeniable positive contributions to growth in the United States except African Americans. Land mines of inequalities planted by histories that are historically false had managed to create false sense of superiority with no basis in fact. The privileged group managed to tilt fact in their favor, and the deprived are left with nothing but destructive, demeaning, and psychologically damaging stories and references that shouldn't have a place in modern society.

Permanent references such as "since slavery" and phrases such as "son of a former slave" designed to preserve the legacy of the shameful and, for the most part, exaggerated stories of slavery are intentionally designed to hold people down in perpetual state of inferiority complex and economic stagnation not designed by God.

There is no doubt this type of references and phrases, reserved for African Americans, has entrapped and held the umbrella of second-class citizens in place. Nothing about the uplifting history of African Americans can be found anywhere. Most people and places believe that those regarded as uplifting stories are nothing but fiction and fairy tale. Those who embarked on constant revelation of them are considered delusional. In reality, nobody ever took the time to look at why do these so-called fiction and fairy-tale uplifting stories keep coming back over and again. These are the stories nobody wants to believe exist or the possibility that there could be some element of truth to them or if there is any reason for the madness of those who believe the stories are credible and true, thereby refusing to let them be swept into oblivion despite the intentional effort of historians and the privileged few to suppress them.

Black institutions or websites, historical facilities and their websites, including Smithsonian, their associates, along with their websites and any organization like them or associated with them are not interested in any of the facts supported by government records. Many of these uplifting histories of African Americans are in the end going to drown out lies and the existing never-ending ocean of misinformation. The demeaning history of slavery disputed by facts is not going to disappear without persistent effort.

The weak and baseless structure of supremacy currently built to encourage hate is going to be dismantled. Oppressors have managed to bury the truth in hopes of never to reveal them! However, the time has come to open the vault of supported facts in favor of revealing the truth and in favor of eliminating any made-up sense of supremacy.

Take a trip to any museum of African American history and you will never find anything in reference to the fact that many of the African Americans (the place was established to inspire) were slave owners of white slaves. You will never find references to any law and statue written, passed, and signed into law in support of the same. You will never find anything in reference to the true and authentic population of African Americans along with the breakdown of the same to justify and support the number of those reported as slaves.

Presenting the facts does not necessarily mean that one group of African American was better than the other. The truth cannot be swept under the carpet because of what was attributed to a few but not all. We are not immature and uncivilized as to have difficulties handling the truth.

The watered-down version of history we are left with insults intelligence and leaves many people wondering was there anything good! Was there anything noble and inspiring in history that can be attributed to African Americans other than the demeaning and self-serving stories of the past developed by the people who believe that they are superior with the help of segregationists only to turn around and called it our stories?

Hate dwells in the pond of misinformation and pride itself in the suppression of facts. Hate will never voluntarily depart from our society as long as the breeding ground is untouched and their baseless hateful rhetoric is allowed to continue.

FOOTPRINT OF HATE

Neo-Nazism grew out of National Socialism commonly known as simply Nazism in Germany. To say that ideology and set of practices of a political party known as Nazi Party can grow to become one of the most effective hate group in history defies logic. However, when you look at the prevalent rate pf race of trying to make an indelible footprint at the expense of others, it is not difficult to imagine. Who could have guessed that there is room in politics for hate?

The National Socialism carefully crafted scientific racism coupled with anti-Semitism influenced by the campaign and the desire for Pan-Germanism gave birth to neo-Nazism and eventually to other organizations such as White Nationalist, Supremacist, Alt-Right, etc. "Neo-Nazi activity" as reported by the *Free Encyclopedia* "is a global phenomenon." The desire to be different is enough to energize hate, thereby help it spread like wildfire.

Erroneous information and assumption is oftentimes difficult to rule out in political ideology. Any leader or influential member of a political party can inject idea or belief that has no basis in fact, most especially if the effort to convince is backed by oratory and out-of-this-world confidence. It is even scarier when the people around those erroneous information and assumption are going out of their ways to defend stupidity. They would do anything to intentionally overlook serious mental health issues along with morally deficient persona of their own leader. They oftentimes pass out dyslexia and pathological lies of the leader as a joke. Those pushing the erroneous information usually do so once they know that they have what look like a solid platform. They are oftentimes obsessed with erroneous and assumed high intelligence quotient (IQ) with no basis in fact. Nothing out of their mouth can be believed because of a never-ending stream of made-up stories delivered with out-of-this-world confidence.

Supremacy, as revealed by *Webster* dictionary, was first used in 1537. It is defined as "the state or condition of being superior to all others in authority, power, or status." The premise and platform on which supremacy was built was mostly subjective. It was never challenged but inadvertently ignored by those who could have shut it down as nothing but bragging and self-glorification. As a result, it spread among those who are obsessed by it and believed that they can make it stick. The word *supremacy* lingered on until it became the watchword of a kingdom and the bedrock of division, prejudice, discrimination and segregation. It later transformed into something bigger, prideful with hateful undertone directed at any opposing views—individual or group.

Historical fact along with validated and available data did not support what the word *supremacy* represents. The word basically did not and still does not have roots in facts. The subjective claim continues, and our generation is forced to grapple with its ever-present baseless and provoking assumptions. A platform designed to deceive the world and promote holier-than-thou attitude in the interest of claiming supremacy is a weak platform and no doubt insult intelligence.

HIDDEN TRUTH

From the record of the United States government kept in the National Achieve of the United States are the following:

> SECTI,O::' 1. *Be it enacted bJ! th- Senate and House of Representatives of.tlte Untted States of Amenca m Congress assembled,* That any alien, <u>being a free white person,</u> who shall have resided within the limits and under the jurisdiction of the United States for the term of two years, may be admitted to become a citizen thereof: on application to any common law court of record, 1Il anyone of the states wherein he shall have resided for the term of one year at least, and making proof to the satisfaction of such court, that he, is a person of good character, and taking the oath or affirmation prescnbed by law, to support the constitution of the United States, which oath or affirmation such court shall administer' and the clerk of such comt shall record such application, and the pro:

Underline of the phrase "being a free white person" is mine. The significance of the phrase is in the fact that it undoubtedly gives a connotation that not all white person (men and women) came to this country as free men and women. Every effort to hide the truth are in what was introduced, passed, and signed into law as well as many information exposed either by the government, various organizations, or individual scholars.

> —— c. 5. " Whereas it has been questioned whether Indians or negroes, manumitted or othewise free, could be capable of purchasing Christian servants, it is enacted that no negro or Indian, though baptized and enjoying their own freedom, shall be capable of any such purchase of Christians, but yet not debarred from buying any of their own nation :" c. 12, " whereas

This government record obtained with the help of the National Achieve indicates that many blacks were slave owners of whites and other ethnic group. Someone must have seen it differently to prompt the introduction of laws, which were eventually passed and signed to stop black ownership of white slaves.

Part of such law previously published in book one of the *Culprit of Division* is hereby shown below:

> It is hereby enacted, That no negros, mulattos, or Indians, although Christians, or Jews, Moors, Mahometans, or other infidels, shall, at any time, purchase any Christian servant, nor any other, expect of their own complexion, or such as are declared slaves by this act: And if any negro, mulatto, or Indian, Jew, Moor, Mahometan, or other infidel, or such as are declared slaves by this act, shall, notwithstanding, purchase *any Christian white servant*, the said servant shall, ipso facto, become free and acquit from any service then due, and shall be so held, deemed, and taken: And if any person, having such Christian servant, shall intermarry with any such negro, mulatto, or Indian, Jew, Moor, Mahometan, or other infidel, *every Christian*

white servant of every such person so intermarrying, shall, ipso facto, become free and acquit from any service then due to such master or mistress so intermarrying, as aforesaid.

And be it further enacted, That no minister of the church of England, or other minister, or person whatsoever, within this colony and dominion, shall hereafter wittingly presume to marry a white man with a negro or mulatto woman; or to marry a white woman with a negro or mulatto man, upon pain of forfeiting and paying, for every such marriage the sum of ten thousand pounds of tobacco; one half to our sovereign lady the Queen, her heirs and successors, for and towards the support of the government, and the contingent charges thereof; and the other half to the informer; To be recovered, with costs, by action of debt, bill, plaint, or information, in any court of record within this her majesty's colony and dominion, wherein no essoin, protection, or wager of law, shall be allowed.

When you hear that George Washington, Hamilton, Thomas Jefferson, and many others like them were all slave owners, history never reveals how many of their slaves were white or any other European ethnic groups and how many of their slaves were Africans. However, the version of history recorded by hate group, which was designed to shame one ethnic group and inspire another, revealed otherwise. Forcing people to own what is not exclusive to them is beyond sinful, it is ungodly. If the stigma and the shameful story of slavery is such that no one wants to identify with it, it's about time we completely erased any reference to slavery from the human history everywhere on earth.

Hate group love phrases such as "son of former slave" only in reference to African Americans exclusively and not to any other ethnic group! It is music to their ears and no doubt help justify their false sense of supremacy. Philanthropists who like to fund the continuum of erroneous history are elated to see African Americans stepped out to claim slavery exclusively.

They are happy and satisfied as long as the truth is suppressed with no intent to ever reveal and expose what is real and true. Many African Americans always like to repackage and relabel inventions of African American as something brought here by slaves. Nothing could be more wrong!

The public, media, and historians are not unaware of so many unsubstantiated misnomers including biases and demeaning character assassinations, vocabularies, terminologies, and phrases that are keeping slavery alive among the children of God. Such phrases as low IQ, prone to violence, unjustified anger, laziness, inability to innovate, addicted to sex, inability to cope with challenges of life, and many others that cannot be mentioned here are music to the ears of every Conan the destroyer everywhere.

Other ethnic groups connected to slavery are happy to see that the world pushed slavery on African Americans and all African American establishments including historical places, individuals as well as institution of learning and religious establishments decided to claim slavery and own it exclusively even when there is nothing in history to support other than the account of the oppressor. By the same token, nothing to prove that all opposing views are wrong other than, also, the self-serving account of the oppressor. They refused to have their names, the names of their ancestors, and history link with the blemish and the dehumanizing history of slavery in the same way as they have done to African Americans.

The destructive stigma left many inspirationally destitute, desolate, dejected, and uninspired, thereby hating themselves and their own kind with passion. Investors and those lucky to be at the forefront of technology does not believe in giving African Americans opportunity through employment or giving them opportunity necessary to showcase their technological know-how or innovation in any area. How do you explain the fact that only 2 percent of Google employees are black? The same goes for other technology companies in the Silicon Valley area and beyond. The question still remains: "How long will prejudice blind the visions of men?"

We all know that the persistent stigma will not go away as long as we are all afraid to confront historically false story and hate necessary to dismantle inferiority complex that has plague the African American communities for generations.

Slavery has been around for thousands of years. However, slavery as we know it today started with the Barbary slave trade of sixteenth century when, as recorded by the United States National Achieve, "the Barbary Coast of North Africa, (the Ottoman provinces of Algeria, Tunisia and Tripolitania along with the independent sultanate of Morocco) frequently raided coastal villages and towns, especially in southern Britain and other European countries to enslave people." This went on for about ninety years before the first African slave trade of Jamestown Virginia in 1619.

Figure 2. White slave trade—the Barbary slave trade in North Africa of sixteenth century

Figure 3. White slave trade of Barbary—North Africa

Figure 4. White slave of Barbary—North Africa

Slavery is a human dilemma—degrading and demeaning story of the past. It is not exclusive to any ethnic group and definitely not black history any more than it is white history. It does not belong in any African American museum and definitely not in any public places in the United States and around the world. It is nothing but a blemish on the human family. It is the devil's way of creating inequality, therefore should not be glorified or dignified in any way shape or form. The historian's desire to continue to push African Americans to singlehandedly bear the shameful and dehumanizing act of slavery, which by itself is appalling, and those who believe it should be ashamed of themselves.

THE MESTIZOS CAME TO THE USA AS SLAVES

How many people knew about slave trade involving the mestizos or Asians hereby labeled "Europeans" and "yellow" respectively? Who made the decision to suppress this important information? How did slavery end up at the doorstep of black people, exclusively, thereby becoming the monkey on the back of black people designed to magnify and uphold the shameful story of the past? The list provided here came from the National Achieve of the United States, and as you can see, it shows blacks, yellow, and the mestizos as slaves. This group was never mentioned anywhere in reference to slavery until now. It makes you wonder, how many other ethnic groups were involved in slavery and no one knew much about them?

Slave Name	Ship	Age	Sex	Class	Slave Residence
Child	Steamboat Hamburgh				
Grace	Steamboat Agusta Brooks	50	Female		Beaufort
Mary	Steamboat Hamburgh	25	Female	Black	Hamburgh
Nanny	Unnamed	50	Female	Yellow	Beaufort
Chloe	Hamburg	20	Female	Yellow	Georgia
Ben	Edgefield	25	Male	Mestizo	Charleston, S.C.
Ruth	Edgefield	60	Female	Black	Charleston, S.C.
Sam	Commerce	27	Male	Black	Charleston, S.C.
Scipio	Edgefield	8 m	Male	Black	Charleston, S.C.
Susan	Hamburg	9 m	Female	Yellow	Georgia
Thomas	Edgefield	15	Male	Mestizo	Charleston, S.C.
Tom	Edgefield	22	Male	Mulato	Charleston, S.C.
Venus	Edgefield	19	Female	Black	Charleston, S.C.

Mestizos are people of combined European and Amerindian or Pacific Islander descent

Figure 5. This information made available after independence
and before the signing of Emancipation Proclamation

A nine-months old "yellow" slave recorded in this table tells me that the nine-month-old was born into slavery. What that means is that his parents were slaves—chattel slaves.

I read *Roots* with an open mind. What a brilliant literary work! The movie that came out of it was extremely touching and genuinely portrayed and highlighted extreme pride-induced wickedness and no doubt showed act of man's inhumanity to man at its iniquitous best. Somehow, *Roots* never revealed the truth about slavery. A lot of books were written and movies produced afterward, but none ever revealed the truth about other ethnic group involved in slavery. There was no reference made anywhere as to the fact that there were so many black slave owners of slaves from different ethnic group before so many laws introduced, passed, and signed to stop the practice.

The misleading information as to the actual number of Africans in captivity came, for the most part, from this piece of information obtained from the State of Virginia database.

The Trans-Atlantic Slave Trade Database has information on almost 36,000 slaving voyages

that forcibly embarked over 10 million Africans for transport to the Americas between the sixteenth and nineteenth centuries. The actual number is estimated to have been as high as 12.5 million. The database and the separate estimates interface offer researchers, students and the general public a chance to rediscover the reality of one of the largest forced movements of peoples in world history.

Before you run with this misleading information, try as much as possible to understand the intricacies with great uncertainties of trying to put together the population of Africa (the source of the so-called forced movement) between the sixteenth and eighteen centuries. Think about the unnecessary assumptions and unsubstantiated estimate that can lead to exaggerated numbers.

Whatever estimated number of Africans in captivity did not take into account other ethnic group involved in the same "forced movement." What was the estimated population of the United States between the sixteenth and nineteenth centuries? That was the highlighted time. You may also want to know the population of Africans precluded by law from purchasing slaves of another ethnic group. How did the 12.5 million from Africa cross the Atlantic Ocean? Where is an estimate with very little deviation and not the exaggerated and fabricated stories with no basis in fact?

The constant reminder of slavery by the media only in reference, exclusively, to African American, in a way, is music to the ears of every hate group. It is also very helpful to their never-ending crusade of false supremacy while disregarding facts. The media is not unaware of the impact of their lies and cover-up of the truth about slavery. They know that a great deal of people was affected on both sides, but they only want to amplify and talk about slavery as it relates to black people and not interested in the slavery of white or any other ethnic group. How do you expect hate, prejudice, inequalities, segregation, and division to come to an end in our world?

"Since slavery" is a misnomer. "Son of a former slave" is a misnomer. Attempt to diminish and dismiss innovation and contributions by black people as "something brought here by slaves" is an intentional attempt to trample on ingenuity. How many times have you heard the media, in reference to white ethnic group, use the phrase "since slavery" or call any white person "son of former slave" or refer to African American as "son of former slave owners"? This blatant disregard of facts is, no doubt, promoting supremacy without telling supremacists, "We got your back." Slavery should not be remembered and does not deserve a place or platform in any society or in any museum.

Nonchalant attitude of the general public along with the willful and deliberate act to continue to pretend like it only happened to one ethnic group is a fuel designed to continue helping the fire of false supremacy and hate. Slavery was an unfortunate thorn and completely evil on so many levels. It was not only meant to dehumanize, it was also meant to divide, segregate, and place one ethnic group above the rest. In a way, it was ungodly.

PARALLEL BETWEEN COLONIZATION AND SLAVERY

Similar to slavery was the colonization of foreign land. Dictionary defines *colonization* as "the action or process of settling among and establishing control over the indigenous people of an area." It also includes "the action of appropriating a place or domain for one's own use" usually against the will and desire of the rightful people of that place or domain.

Just like slavery, a handful of countries managed to avoid colonization, thereby escaping the demeaning and painful aspect of complete takeover by foreign power of what rightfully belongs to a different group of people and considered as sovereign land. Some of you would be shocked to learn that Britain, the emperor of colonization (who got into colonization in the interest of trade expansion and not for military might), was once colonized by many foreign powers such as the Normans, the Vikings, the Jutes, Picts, Anglos, and Saxons and after that the Romans. The earliest considered as prehistoric settlement of the British Isles was by the Celts. Although some would like to argue that because Scotland was once occupied but not colonized means Britain was never colonized. Nothing could be further from the truth.

There were only eleven countries never colonized by foreign powers but suffered the dominant influence of occupiers. They are as following:

1. Ethiopia, a country once occupied by Italy but was never colonized.
2. Liberia was a settlement of an African American who decided to go back to the motherland.
3. China was briefly occupied by Mongolia under the leadership of Genghis Khan or Chinggis Khaan (1162–1227). Genghis as he was popularly known was born Temüjin, the founder of the Mongol Empire. He became a force to be reckoned with after he managed to unite many of the nomadic tribes of Northeast Asia. However, China was never colonized.
4. Bhutan
5. Nepal
6. Afghanistan
7. Thailand
8. Korea
9. Japan
10. Iran
11. Saudi Arabia—once occupied but not colonized.

If you think you are immune to any of the greediness of the past, think again. If you think that you or your ethnic group were never subject to any of the unfair demeaning treatment of the past, think again. Perhaps it happened once, but it happened

It does not matter what was presumed to be true. It does not matter how the truth got twisted in favor of misinformation. It does not matter what was assumed and for how long. What matters is what was suppressed and why. What matters is the fact that the truth, although suppressed was not destroyed. I do not need unscientific research, hearsay, unsubstantiated stories passed on from generation to generation including bias and patronizing public opinion built on "cultural anxiety" and differences designed only to help the privileged group in their bid to rule the world.

If all I have to establish the truth is individual opinion or interpretation, the purpose of establishing culprit of division is dead on arrival. It is, no doubt, highly required of me to give you authentic blueprint that was ignored by all organizations and historians until now. If you believe that you have convincing information to disprove everything in this chapter, do not hesitate to reveal. If you disagree with anything in this book and you believe that you are eloquent enough to destroy the truth, do not hesitate to come forth. Bring whatever document or law from credible sources or bring your rhetoric and your convincing power of eloquence and let's put this conversation in front of the people for necessary scrutiny. The same is extended to any members of the media or historical organizations with disputing information to come forth.

The fact, as revealed by some of the information received from the National Achieve, that "African laborers were more suitable than European and Indigenous laborers as they used to working in tropical agricultural conditions, eating tropical foods, and were resistant to European diseases," does not present enough reason for enslavement and the distortion of historical facts.

INACCURACIES AND FALSEHOOD

Failure of institutions, lawmakers, and government to correct misinformation and bring back lost pride, civility, and inspiration to all of God's children necessitate that we step back and look at some of the stigmas, mind-crippling and anger-provoking shame carefully crafted and forced on one ethnic group in the interest of what is pleasing and satisfying to nearly the rest of the human family.

Hate aimed at any disadvantaged group or persons is more acceptable, justifiable, and in some cases easy to quickly dismiss as inconsequential than address, condemn, and rectify it. Hate group will never stop as long as they are under the illusion that they are no longer on the receiving end of whatever legacy and stigma of the past. Segregation and division perpetrated on a substantial number of the human family as a result of hate will never be effectively dealt with until we all agree, stand up, and say with one voice, "Enough is enough," thereby change inaccuracies and falsehood.

What do we really know about slavery as existed in fifteenth all the way to the eighteenth centuries? The Internet is full of explanation that simply does not explain anything but add more fuel to the fire of confusion. Many of the effort to explain slavery and who was actually enslaved leave more questions than answered. Some of the explanations given to justify the enslavement of "them" and not "us" insults intelligence in every way and encourages a deeper gulf of division. If the truth exposed does not conform to the thinking of whoever feels like defending false history, the next unsolicited action is usually to classified whatever is available as either lies or myth. They are more comfortable in "that is your problem and not ours" idiosyncratic and holier-than-thou attitude.

Some of the explanations provided and currently available include two different and supposedly distinct types of slavery. One classified slavery as "hereditary chattel slavery" and the other as simply "indentured servants."

CONTRADICTORY EXPLANATIONS

The general explanations provided by those who like to pin the story of slavery on blacks only is that those brought from Africa are basically regarded as "hereditary chattel slaves." In that case, they are considered properties with no human rights and no freedom to do as they wish regardless of who was here prior to slavery and who came as a result of slavery, hence the insensitive and demeaning generalized reference of the United States of America media such as "son of former slave." The most important question still remains unanswered and that is, how do you know he was a "son of former slaves" and not son of a former slave owner?

Those black people were further classified as subhuman or in some cases "nonhuman" that cannot be included in important data such as census (population count). Input from them as to how they should live their lives is regarded as unimportant. Many deranged scientists opened the dehumanizing windows to justify this type of sick way to segregate the human family and to solidify the stupid projection of false sense of superiority.

Part of the new argument is that many other ethnic groups brought to the Americas were merely "indentured servant" and that the word *slaves* in reference to those viewed as "indentured servant" was merely derogatory and not real. They trained their minds to believe that all black people in the Americas came as a result of "chattel slavery." However, what took place did not agree with this self-serving divisive and highly neglectful and unintelligent argument of the bigots who somehow believe that shaming others will in the end boost their dim-witted and unjustified ego.

Let us take a careful look at those whites chained and brought from Europe against their will. Many of them were sold to the highest bidder in an open market. If a person is offered up for sale, bought, and owned by another human being, that constitutes as slavery. This, unfortunately, happened to many whites as well as some blacks in the Americas beginning from the fifteenth century and even before. What happened to the nineteen Africans in Virginia in 1619 had happened to a lot of Irish including other white ethnic group prior to 1619 and remained so for so many years thereafter. No matter how you look at it, slavery is slavery and the memory of it deserve to be erased from everywhere.

The other version of history most would like to suppress forever reveals the fact that many Africans who bought and owned Irish and many other Europeans as slaves have been doing it prior to the enslavement of Africans in the Americas. I am not proud of this deplorable history and egregious dehumanizing behaviors practiced among the human family. I have to make reference to it in the interest of establishing fact that we were all on the same boat.

If the goal of those who does not want to remember the enslavement of Irish and other white is to erase that fact from history, the word *slavery* in reference to any African Americans should be equally stricken and erased from history and from our society, from any classroom, from our vocabularies and everyday interactions in the interest of peaceful coexistence. This, by itself, is the main reason for hate—the undisputed fertile land and culprit of division. There is no other way to describe it.

Any act involving buying and selling of another human being, past and present, constitutes slave trade pure and simple. It does not matter how you try to explain it or justify it; what is shameful is shameful and should be removed not just from one ethnic group but among the children of God. There is no place for the word *slaves* or *slavery* in our society.

FACTS:

1. Many Africans in the Americas and most especially in the United States were slave owners of white slaves
2. "Enslavement of Caucasians was 'finally' banned in the early 19th century, while slaves from other groups were allowed"
3. The argument developed to prove systemic "hereditary chattel slavery" although true in reference to a few but categorically false in reference to all. Many of what took place simply did not support this insensitive argument.

4. There were free Africans who owned slaves that are blacks. Nothing could be further from the truth. Many free Africans who stepped forward to buy some of the few that were held in slavery did so to free them. If anything, free Africans outright rejected enslavement of another African in the interest of the fact that they regarded each other as brothers and sisters, hence the birth of the word *brother* in reference to one another

Part of the problem with the half-truth argument currently available in the history class and on the Internet is the fact that many of them are written to the exclusive neglect of credible fact. This part of their argument prompted me to reexamine one of the laws passed in search of the logic behind some of the restrictions placed on Africans. Real legislations passed, signed, and adopted reveal the truth. I just have to question some of the explicit language of some of those past laws. None of the laws support the argument that all African Americans came here as a result of "chattel slavery" as we were made to believe. If you do not have access to some of the laws in question, try and obtain volume one of the *Culprit of Division*. Some are published there. The fact that not all Africans who came here came to this land as a result of slavery remains indelible in fact. The fact that many came as explorers and sojourners remains undisputed. Not only that,

1. many African American were proud slave owners of white slave— Irish, German and even English slaves.
2. in 1705, and a few years thereafter, many laws passed here in the United States to stop those Africans from having slaves of another ethnic group. This is nowhere to be found in any history book

QUESTIONS:

a. If the demeaning assumption that they all came here as chattel slaves was true, how did they manage to become slave owners in light of the fact that chattel slaves are properties with no rights and no freedom?

b. If they never owned slaves in any way, shape, or form as that agent of hate, would have you believe, why was the law written to prevent them from having slaves of another ethnic group?

c. If the law was semantic based on assumption designed to curb the possibility that African American slave owners could be true, why was that necessary? Has any law ever passed based on speculations and not on reality?

ERRONEOUS ASSUMPTION:

3. George Washington, Hamilton, and many others like them, although slave owners but how many of their slaves were white and how many of them were yellow or black or any other ethnic group?

4. According to the information obtained from the Library of Congress, the population of Africans in the US in 1790 was less than a million. That tells me that the population of Africans in 1690 was just a few and perhaps less than or around one hundred. Where is any concrete information to support the assumption that millions of African slaves were transplanted from Africa to the New World?

5. According to the estimated population of Africa in 1690, the population of the entire continent of Africa was around 15 million during the slave trade. Where is any concrete information to support the assumption that 12.5 million Africans were brought to the New World as chattel slaves?

Whites are not the only ethnic group endowed to enjoy pride in the people they are. Africans were deprived of their pride and uplifting part of their history. They were forced to own, exclusively, history of slavery that was not exclusive to them, why? References such as "son or daughter of a former slave" in reference to African American is nothing but a misnomer created by hate group. Why was it that this was never corrected? If we are ever going to erase hate and division, the deplorable history we inherited must be erased.

DIVISION AND RECENT/ONGOING SETBACK

Some of what we are witnessing today such as the 2015 church massacre in Charleston, South Carolina, and the 2017 peaceful march against hate turned violence in Charlottesville, Virginia, is not the beginning and unfortunately will not be the end. The young lady who died and lost such a precious life in Charlottesville, Heather Heyer, did not die in vain.

Those who were injured exercising their right to protest for right did not suffer in vain. It is not against the law to protest. Effort designed to ridicule and smear a highly qualified, legitimate, and democratically elected president of the United States is not the beginning and possibly will not be the end. Defamation of character aimed at LeBron James is not the beginning and not likely to be the end. The president of the United States (an individual elected by the people to serve the people) calling peaceful African American football players who were merely exercising their rights "sons of bitches," is not the beginning and probably will not be the end. Hate needs to be defeated!

Recent discriminatory law known as Senate Bill 43 passed, signed, and adopted in Missouri is not the beginning and surely will not be the end. Hate is not going to pack up and depart voluntarily from our world without the tireless effort of many peace-loving, God-fearing, and upright members of the human family.

The confederacy and all its branches such as the Ku Klux Klan, Alt-right, neo-Nazi, and white supremacists descended on the city of Charlottesville, Virginia, to remind people that hate is still very much alive. They wanted to impress on the public the fact that they are not going to willingly drop hate and any act of violence. They and their biggest cheerleader, the hater and divider in chief, President Trump, are morally deficient and simply do not understand what compassion, bringing people together, or inclusiveness is all about.

The hate group are fighting for what they consider as their land and the need for those who look like them to rule the world. They believe that they are the only legitimate people with exclusive right to this world and what the world has to offer. If you think they are crazy, you could be right! But there is a hidden desire in their demand; there is a reason for their madness. As I said before, their goal is to preserve what they considered as their possession. The Bible says, "The thieves cometh but to steal, to kill and to destroy."

With that said, let us take a moment to evaluate what we are experiencing:

1. They are concerned about exclusive right to whatever part of the world they think belong to them.
2. Human lives means nothing.
3. The fear of the Lord is not of concern to them.
4. Their hearts are hardened; do not try to change them, you will discover it is highly impossible.
5. They are not open to or receptive to the voice of reason.
6. It does not matter what God say about loving your neighbors. They cannot love you unless you are like-minded.
7. They are full of both concealed and gratuitous hate.

The footprint of hate indelible in their actions speaks volume. Their eyes radiate indignation and resentment only hate can produce. Their rhetoric elevates evil to a new height. To call them racist is a misnomer. They are, without mincing word, workers of iniquity. They are like stain or blemish on the human family.

UNJUSTIFIED ANGER

What we have seen in the past and still experiencing calls for action. No doubt about that! We cannot pretend and act like we are not concerned. We cannot continue to pretend and act like we are not on the same boat or concerned about one another. Indifference is the new weapon of mass destruction.

Hate entered our world, set us against one another, and left us with an unprecedented division and resentment. Series of laws before and after helped nurtured and kept it growing. The world could no longer see the beauty and strength of Africa because of the fact that whatever is left is smeared with incomprehensible blemish and disgust. It is amazing that there are still some people bold enough to call themselves black or identify with Africa.

Some black people in India, Bangladesh, or elsewhere in Asia do not believe they are black but Asians or whatever national or continental identity they prefer. One simple truth is that national or continental identity does not change the color of your skin. Blacks in Africa are the same as blacks in Asia, Europe, America, or elsewhere around the world. The color of your skin is what makes you black or white and not the texture of your hair. For a black India man to say that he pretended to be black defies logic.

The individual who stuck his neck out and wrote a book about this is a black man from India and not Africa. He had forgotten that he is not black because of outward characteristics. In his case, the color of his skin does not permit him to pass as white or yellow since there is no skin color known as Asian. This individual is actually darker than most people from many parts of Africa. He is not light enough to be described as "brown" and not light enough to be called "yellow." He needs to understand that the sugary false sense of different-from-them because of one insignificant characteristic is another way of authenticating baseless segregation. Being Asian has nothing to do with the color of your skin.

Another segregating evidence of the prejudice few as well as diabolical scientist who are wasting their time looking for differences is in the magnification of what some might consider as abnormalities such as longer hands, thick bones, uncommon height and weight, including deep or thin voice and behaviors. These are some of the people you can find in every culture and creed that, for the most part, makes these few members of the human family different from the rest. When a doctor says, "Your child is not normal," it could be that the doctor is looking for unusual growth or abnormalities that can be surgically removed or it could be that the doctor is trying to justify some sick and discriminating research outcome that put your child among different spices. If you hear that your child is not normal, it is always good to ask, "What does that mean?" Be sure to listen attentively to rule out uncharacteristic annoying and highly divisive assumptions.

We are divided against one another in every way possible. To deny the fact about who you are (black or white) is to continue to subscribe to misinformation and worldwide segregation and inexplicable division currently responsible for greater discord and the reason to want to fight and wipe each other out from the face of earth.

Those who still believe that the breath of God keeps our lungs breathing for His glory will forever continue to allow His love, compassion, and kindness to reign supreme in their lives.

USA 2.0: THE REVIVAL OF HATE

There is a new general in charge. What Robert Lee started is now in the hand of a new general masquerading himself as, presumably, an experienced businessman and erroneously accepted as naïve and novice politician who is now the leader of the Free World—a world that is involving. This is an individual who campaigned on the idea of "I alone can fix it." To say that he is naïve is assuming too much and giving so much latitude. To ignore secret agenda deeply rooted and grounded in concealed hate is like jumping into crocodile-infested lake, hoping to swim and come out alive!

No one knew that the United States was indeed a divided nation until the "voice" of hate emerged and every hate group you can imagine started to come out from the woodwork. Their plan to turn "We the people" into "Us the people" and weed out every opposing view and those who are different from them found a new ally in a new presidential candidate who later became the nominee of his party and eventually the president of the United States.

The land of the free and the home of the brave turned into the land of the restricted, isolated, and the home of the constraint. The leader of the Free World is beginning to lose its grip on reality and did not hesitate to turn his back on allies of the United States. Not only that, if the hate group aspiring to further divide should have their way, the United States would become the land of the careless, the land of the "Me first," the land where what God wants is unimportant as long as we are able to get what we want, the land where you are on your own, the land where your government can no longer assist you but take away your rights as well as the freedom and other things you had enjoyed for so long.

The land of the free is now in the hand of a bully who is not afraid to limit or completely stop all social interactions. Everything is in the hand of a would-be dictator ready to use upright and unsuspecting citizens who are blindly following him to advance his secret agenda. Voting right is under review. Freedom to come to the land of immigrant is under fierce attack. Freedom of the press is about to become a thing of the past. Freedom of speech is on its way out, and the right to protest for right, which is undeniably one of the backbones of the United States of America, is about to be scrubbed from the face of earth.

Hate groups are once again marching with guns, torches, and clubs of any kind, knives and even Molotov cocktail. We are looking at a perilous time. Hate is trying to make a comeback. Hate is struggling to rear its ugly head by looking for a way back into the midst of the human family like we have never seen before.

These are no longer farmers (men and women of the Confederacy) looking for a way to drag and force other ethnic group to do work in their farms without paying for services rendered. These are no longer people hoping to hold others in bondage, which is what the Confederate soldiers did in the beginning. They are now your mechanics, dentists, security guards, nurses, teachers, firefighters, lawyers, law enforcement officers, accountants, construction workers, system analysts, software engineers, journalists, network administrators, including many people from all walks of life (employed and unemployed).

They are in neo-Nazi, KKK, white nationalist, supremacist, alternative right, and any kind of hate group you can imagine. They are not unaware that nothing can be done without capturing the citadel of power. Nothing can be done without a passionate sympathizer and hard-core ally who, at the executive branch, is the president of the United States of America, an individual who is not afraid to twist facts to justify inaccuracies or create fake news to smear the real deal as fake. They needed a leader in the Oval Office who is not afraid to vehemently attack the media or any other entity of creating and spreading fake news when in reality, the president himself is the source of most fake news.

Inaccurate information (lies) is the fuel the fire of hates needs to spread like inferno. Inaccurate information is primarily based on what the mind is trained to believe and hold as the truth. The mind of the president is trained to believe his made-up stories which were, no doubt, the reason for his prominent rise to the status of what appeared to be an experienced and well-informed businessman.

Needless to say, the entire hate group found a perfect ally in a person duly elected forty-fifth president of the United States, Donald J. Trump, who became the fake news in chief after his rise to power. Part of the fake news in chief's strategies was to label other people as crooked before anyone can peel off his deeply complicated many layers only to discover no one is more crooked than the man himself. An individual who is not afraid to openly express his disdain, resentment and contempt of all the allies of the United States of America all around the world while openly embrace adversaries, dictators and foes. Why is this really important to highlight?

Unified intelligence from around the world is like having eyes, ears and maintaining physical presence all over the world in hope of detecting unsuspecting attack still in the works before it become a formidable, catastrophic and seriously destructive, and life-threatening attack. To go after allies as well as intelligence communities cannot be seen as simply isolated political actions with nothing sinister intended. It is indeed part of a bigger picture.

The intent to isolate the United States of America goes deeper than just political rhetoric and baseless economic concerns. If the Free World can be successfully fragmented, isolated and political structure at home can be effectively turned against itself through actions that can be explained as inconsequential and similar to actions previously taken by some former leaders, the foundation for the destruction of a high magnitude would have been successfully laid. If the intent to carefully dismantle the United States by attacking all the power players in Washington regardless of political affiliation, and if the freedom of expression including freedom of the press intentionally allowed in the constitution to expose is curtailed, the foundation for one of the most ruthless dictatorship the world had ever seen would have been completed.

Don't let anyone fool you! "Draining the swamp" is actually a higher aim at the three branches of government necessary to create effective "checks and balances." The secret agenda was to attack each structure and those presumably important keepers of the structures. There is no desire to walk across the aisle, across political line to make friends, or convince anyone using some out-of-this-world deal-making skills. He simply does not have any. His modus operandi had always been scare tactics and intimidation designed to force people to submit or give up as opposed to cooperate. If anyone resists, the desire to attack and replace whoever resists and disagrees in the interest of total grip on power is an ever-present option.

Hate is no longer interested in becoming a regional force to be reckoned with but a formidable national and international power player ready to, once again, disrupt the affairs of men and further divide the human family. Hate, which started in the South, has secretly and methodically spread to every nook and cranny of the United States. The cancer is getting bigger and stronger. If you think that they are simply blowing steam in the effort to resurrect something that is dead and gone, you are mistaken. Humanity is once again living in perilous time.

How do you explain the presence of several thousands (not a handful) members of hate groups who suddenly showed up in one city alone chanting, "We want our streets back, we want our cities back. Jews will not replace us"? What does that tell you? If that many people can show up in one city, is it fair to say that there are probably millions of them currently scattered all over this great land known as the United States of America. They have been relatively quiet for many years while operating under the radar until a presidential candidate came out, boldly declared without hesitation, saying, "I am your voice." That's all that was needed for them to come out in record number, declaring that "we want our country back!"

Was there any secret nationalist agenda behind Trump's candidacy? Whose idea was it to curtail immigration and possibly embark on mass deportation of immigrants? Who developed the strategy to seriously attack the media and make the Republican establishment a toothless bulldog? Where is the idea of "our streets" or "our country" coming from? Whose land is this, and who is qualified to use the word *ours?*"

Erratic behaviors can only spring up through erratic leaders who couldn't care less about facts, a leader who is neurotic and unyielding in his effort to twist the truth. In a nutshell, a pathological liar with a lot of undiagnosed mental health issues! If anything, no active president would be willing to submit to psychological or psychiatric evaluation—it can only be done by health-care professionals through evaluation of actions (past and present), words, and deeds plus any other information collected from his interactions with people along with his written responses and information available elsewhere.

Present statistics reveals that we now have a president spewing out, without hesitation, such incredibly alarming lies and inaccurate information with no basis in fact and no desire to correct them once they are proven wrong or debunked, and even if they are proven in a court of law as unsubstantiated and dismissed as such. As reported by CNN, "Trump, within eleven months, has made 1,950 misleading or simply false claims since being sworn in as president on January 20, 2017. That's an average of 5.6 a day." Furthermore, they asserted that "Trump lies with zero sense of shame, guilt or remorse. Unlike most politicians who, when caught in a falsehood or a lie, won't repeat it again for fear of backlash. Trump seems to revel in saying things that have been proven not to be true." What else do we need to establish something pathological? The following are just a few examples (a drop in the bucket) of some lies put out there by the US President Donald J. Trump himself:

1. Story of bullets in pig's blood to silence Islamic radicals—false, never happened.
2. Story that a democratically elected president of the United States was not born in the United States—completely fabricated and dismissed by many as too discriminatory.
3. Wire-tapping of his residence before and after the election—never happened.
4. Inauguration crowds as the largest crowd ever—completely made up.
5. James Comey's tape he talked about for weeks only to discover none existed anywhere.
6. Evidence of undocumented voters in the last election—false.
7. Violence on both sides of protest—no basis in fact.
8. Alleging that there are good people on the side of hate—none existed.

9. Not willing to call those who came to peaceful protest with guns, clubs, and knives including Molotov cocktails domestic terrorists—we are still waiting.

10. How about the false and made-up story that Trump brought back and made "Merry Christmas" fashionable again. None of the former presidents ever stopped saying "Merry Christmas." There is no law in the United States against saying "Merry Christmas"

11. An individual who would go as far as to post fake *Time* magazine's man of the year cover photos at many of his hotels and resorts just to show off fake recognitions.

12. Made-up story of political opponent's dad involvement in the assassination of a president—innuendo.

What else do we need to establish something pathological, diabolical, and extremely divisive from someone expected to lead with sound mind? What about some of his base? Some of their demands include the following:

1. The desire to take our country back.
2. To reclaim our streets.
3. To never allow minorities and foreigners to take our jobs, not realizing that many of the companies were established by the so-called minorities and foreigners.
4. Not to allow Jews to replace them in the land of "We the People," of which all ethnic group labored, fought, and died for.

INJUSTICE AND INEQUALITY MISCONSTRUED

The only country expected to be truly united is gradually becoming one of the most divided countries on the planet. For a democratically elected president of the Free World to openly come out against the people he was elected to govern without making the effort to try to understand the rationale behind their discontent defies logic. To openly call those peaceful protesters "sons of bitches" who deserves to be kicked out of their professions or fired speaks volume.

Neo-Nazis, members of the KKK, the white nationalists, supremacists, the Alt-rights, and every hate group still breathing in the United States came out with intent to inflict pain, if possible, and the same President of the United States called them "good people." Is this what he meant by making "America great again"? Is there any iota of greatness in division? Are we dealing with the intent to purge, separate, and divide? What is going on in the United States leaves us with more questions than answers.

A lot of upright citizens of the United States (black and white) proudly love and openly display the flag of the United States on their properties every day, every week, every month, and every year. Go to the military—Navy, Air Force, Army, Marine, Coast Guard and even law enforcement—and you will come across men and women of the United States (black and white) fighting and defending "the land of the free and home of the brave." To dismiss the important contributions of all Americans in favor of giving false credit to one ethnic group is a slap in the face of patriotism and unity. The United States is already a great nation, and we all have a stake at the greatness of America, and nothing is more important.

Why is it so difficult to understand that protesting injustice and inequalities does not translate into disrespect and disdain for the "flag," "national anthem," or for the "military?" President of the United States is supposed to unite and not divide; but unfortunately, we have divider in chief at the Oval Office, and nothing makes him happier than to set everyone against one another.

Could it be that part of the desire to "make America great again" includes a secret code to law enforcement officers as to how to react to minorities?

USA ELECTION: MEDDLING AND COLLUSION

United States was like a pine on the top of a hill. His greatness was the envy of the world. His military might is like no other. His number one place in technological discovery and exploration in many uncharted territories along with the freedom to innovate helped made the United States a great nation. In the land of immigrants, past immigrants have contributed immensely and new immigrants continue to prove that they too are not here for handouts.

The United States was built on the foundation of inclusiveness—the only nation with a unique slogan of "We the people." Her constitution is like a solid rock built on the idea of never to allow tyranny, persecution, and division to destroy the very foundation many people were glad exist to provide safe haven for every lover of freedom. The same constitution provides a shield from allowing anyone including the president of the United States to embark on dictatorial method of governance, thereby deviating from the very foundation that made the United States a unique nation in many respects.

No government official, law enforcement officers, or politician is allowed to tramp on the right and freedom of citizens of the United States. Freedom to worship, express yourself as well as the freedom of the press is all guaranteed within the constitution of the United States. If you are elected by majority, you still have a duty to serve those who did not vote for you as well as those who voted for you. Outcome of an election cannot be seen as a referendum against you or the one with the least vote but an expression of voters' opinion for or against with no disdain intended and without malice or lasting animosity in any way, shape, or form.

The three branches of government—executive, judicial, and legislative—although operate independently, are expected to work together without trying to nullify the importance of the other. The constitution does not allow the executive branch to exercise unreasonable power over the rest. There is no provision in the constitution of the United States for absolute power but a system of checks and balances. If anything, members of the executive branch are expected to not engage in personal business while carrying out their civic duties to avoid conflict of interest. Their interactions with foreign government are not expected to be personally beneficial and financially rewarding to them. Nothing is expected to lead to conflict of interest and they are expected to put the interest of the United States first regardless of any admiration they might have for any foreign government. They are expected to let our adversaries know that the priorities and interests of the United States as well as the full protection of democracy around the world are nonnegotiable and cannot be compromised.

The need to respect each other's role is of utmost importance for the smooth operation of the government. To publicly criticize or attack a group such as the intelligence communities or any department such as the department of justice or a subdivision of it such as the FBI to the point of demoralizing them is, no doubt, un-American and completely unacceptable. It opens the door for any foreign government, entity, or individual to ridicule and poke fun. The law allows disciplinary action against one rotten egg in a group or department. That is something that is not unexpected and cannot be ruled out, but to intentionally and publicly disgrace or demoralize a group or department is unacceptable

All these branches as well as their subordinate branches, offices, and department at the federal, state, and municipal level are expected to respect each other autonomy and jurisdictions in the interest of making sure the nation is protected and that people are safe and secure in their own homes. The role of those using their talent to help us relax and unwind through entertainment of various kind cannot be marginalized and minimized.

Those in the media, institution of learning, various religious organization, in agriculture, manufacturing, technology, medical, various businesses as well as those making sure the helpless and the hopeless are not forgotten deserve their rightful place at the podium of recognition.

The role of the commander in chief as the cheerleader in chief, the consoler in chief, the unifier in chief cannot be forgotten. To be the commander in chief, the man or woman at the apex of power, the president who is elected to occupy the Oval Office is to not put ethnic leaning ahead of public interest. His or her ethnicity, skin color, creed, culture. and political leaning should fade into the background as the leader of "We the People." If you have not seen it before, you need to know and believe the truth that is "self-evident that all men are created equal." President is expected to "become all things to all people" bring people together, thereby continuing on the foundation laid by the founding fathers.

It is expected of the commander in chief to stand up for democracy all around the world and to put the interest of the United States above all things including self-interest and admiration existing or perceived of any foreign leaders whose political agenda, interest, and goal are in direct opposite of that of the United States. No politician is expected to put American's life in danger directly or indirectly and definitely not the president of the United States. Inability to condemn the human right abuse of adversary along with inability to stand up for Democracy around the world constitutes collusion with evil. Inability to impose sanction approved by the legislative branch constitutes collusion. Inability to call out a leader whose grip on power makes it impossible for people to express themselves openly without reprisal of any kind, a leader whose idea of freedom are for those who admire him and worship the very ground he or she walks on constitute collusion. In the United States, these types of collusions are a crime.

Collusion, according to *Webster's* dictionary, is defined as cooperation especially for an illegal or deceitful purpose. Collusion as a conspiracy also include conspiring with the enemy. Either way, collusion is a crime. When the hardened enemy of freedom and democracy step forward to offer dirt on opponent, normal response should have been, no we are not interested. The intent to entertain such unsolicited assistance constitutes collusion, therefore opens the door with full cooperation and agreement to commit crime.

The need to establish fact arises, most especially, when explicit collusion and implicit collusion are pretty much present and proven to exist. During one of his campaign stops in Doral, Florida, Donald J. Trump as reported by Ashley Parker and David E. Sanger on July 27, 2016, said "that he hoped Russian intelligence services had successfully hacked Hillary Clinton's e-mail, and encouraged them to publish whatever they may have stolen, essentially urging a foreign adversary to conduct cyber espionage against a former secretary of state." When he said that, he was explicitly soliciting for cooperation from a well-known adversary of the United States—a foreign power considered enemy of freedom and democracy. His call was not ignored and did not fall on deaf ears; he got what he asked for and that constitutes collusion, which is a crime.

An open invitation to Russia by Donald J. Trump was an irresistible special invitation designed to reward them for their effort. We now see it as meddling, but a meddling responding to a special invitation sent out by a legitimate candidate running for the highest office in the land. It was irresistible in many ways. In this case, Russia is an unwilling participant tempted to act. Whether this was a deviation from their original mission is still left to be seen. Nevertheless, this constitute implicit collusion which is a crime. I don't want you to think that Trump's invitation to Russia was ambiguous or a joke, it was not. It connotes intended compensation if the information exposed is useful.

When an individual described as Russia's lawyer along with several others met with Donald Trump Jr. to offer damaging information on the opponent and Trump Jr. entertained the idea, he and his entourage implicitly engaged in collusion which is a crime.

Involvement of Russia was so important to Donald J. Trump; he avoided publicly criticizing them or condemning their action in the election of 2016. It was also important to Trump that he had to refuse to implement the sanction approved by the legislative branch. He was not reluctant in admonishing his own intelligence communities and making an effort to demoralize the Federal Bureau of Investigation (FBI) along with the Department of Justice as well as publicly attack anyone who tried to unveil his love for his bedfellow—Russia. He did not hold back in his effort to consistently blame his predecessor President Barrack Obama for his own (Donald J. Trump) unwillingness to take action and his own incompetency. This type of passive attitude constitutes collusion and explicit collusion for that matter.

There have been many inconsistencies, cover-ups, denial, and many never-ending lies about what actually took place. What else do we need to establish collusion? The intent to sow the seed of discord set the citizens of the United States against one another and isolate the United States from the rest of the world is obvious in all actions and deed of the current president who is not afraid to blame his predecessor for his own inability to govern and his willingness to defend Russia at every opportunity available to him.

The United States' role as the conscience of the world and the touch bearer for Democracy, freedom, and the rule of law as well as full protection for Americans including full protection for our allies and friendly nations should be part of the goals of the president of the United States. United States is not a nation expecting to walk away from those seeking freedom regardless of where they are from. The need to help anyone from around the world seeking to enjoy liberty and the pursuit of happiness is nonnegotiable. Collusion, in any way, with hostile foreign government considered as adversary of the United States can be seen as a crime, more so if the collusion fails to condemn abuse of human rights and infliction of unspeakable pain including death on all opposing voices in the home country of the adversary.

If you have an individual like Paul Manafort with back-end and front-end connection to Russia as your campaign chairman and not afraid to stick his neck out in the interest of what is beneficial to Russia along with willful intent to engage in criminal activities, which he hoped no one would ever find out, how can you say there was no collusion? Paul was there communicating with key players in the invasion of Ukraine, which led to the annexation of Crimea. As a double representative who was not afraid to hide compensation (money paid for his services) with regard to Ukraine affairs along with money paid to others in connection to the same from been detected, how can we say it is difficult to establish explicit collusion? What was he telling the major player in the invasion of Ukraine and the annexation of Crimea about the Trump campaign?

To understand this better, why would Russia choose to publicly support Trump's campaign as opposed to Clinton's campaign? When you see a possible incoming administration, who is not afraid to object to expand your influence around the world in a way that creates pain at home and abroad, you are prone to support the lesser of the two evils. When you discover that one of the two running for the top position in the only country likely to make the so-called expansion of influence a little difficult for you to achieve, you are bound to support the one willing to look the other way while you aggressively go out in pursuit of expanding your influence and territory. Once the support is established, you are bound to find a way to the main candidate to let him know that we got your back. In that wise, the chairman of Trump's campaign decided to be the link—the middleman and the executioner. How can we say there is no explicit collusion?

The desire to set the United States on collision course with major allies all around the world was designed to isolate the United States, distract and divert the attention of the legislative branch from digging into whatever was going on. It is also a blatant intent to distract and divert the attention of the press and the intelligence communities from focusing and exposing what was going on. The intent to recklessly go after the press as creating fake news and also to demoralize the intelligence communities constitute implicit collusion.

The possibility of looking into nepotism as unacceptable behavior on the part of any government official including the president is enough to keep any descent and law-abiding citizen wide awake at night. It is much more dangerous when the individual likely to be accused of nepotism fails to receive clearance necessary to give him access to unclassified information continue to receive briefing and unrestrained access to classified information. To allow Jared Kushner to have full access to foreign dignitaries to the extent of soliciting loan or investment in his business of which the president may or may not have personal interest is the kind of access that can be seen, at a minimum, as colluding with foreign government. It is difficult to not expect something in return. What about a promise to not focus on your activities within the United States or in regard to the United States? What if the so-called foreign investor or loan company is working on behalf of a third-party government, in a way, likely to derail Democracy or lead to major discord within the United States as well as within her allies? In that case, we are looking at implicit collusion. Every gift, investment, and loan received should be scrutinized to eliminate impropriety.

Trump administration is not interested in investigating the cyberattack perpetrated on the United States during the election of 2016 in order to prevent such from happening again. Nothing could be more dangerous, catastrophic, and, if allowed, would swiftly move beyond election meddling into other areas such as technological and military development. Protecting Democracy is not a top priority for Trump as much as protecting his complicated financial dealings. As the only one who is fully aware of existing collusion within his campaign during the election, he is not afraid to have things remain buried forever. When personal interest is more important than national interest or the need to protect Democracy around the world, no amount of convincing would lead to expected result.

Vladimir Putin cannot be made a scapegoat in this case. His primary goal is to expand Russia's influence around the world. Regardless of any distraction, he remains focused. His desire to penetrate the United States and attack him from within through planting the seed of discord remains uncompromised. His intent to do to the United States what they did to the Soviet Union was too much for Mr. Putin to ignore. When you look very carefully into the action of Mr. Putin, you cannot but admire his consistency, ability to remain focus, and his plan to make sure Russia is not relegated to the level of regional super power but a global superpower and a force to be reckoned with. In one of his display of military might, Mr. Putin was quoted as saying, "We cannot be ignored anymore."

Another way to achieve his goal is to create unprecedented gulf of division between the United States and his ally nations around the world and to eventually isolate the United States. Mr. Putin understands that it might be difficult to achieve that kind of desire without a willing soul in the White House, and that willing soul is the current president—Donald J. Trump. Unfortunately, no president in the United States can rule beyond the dictate of the Constitution of the United States. Totalitarian, dictatorial, or limitless rule is not allowed. In that case, Donald J. Trump's days are numbered, and any executive order not in favor of the United

States or not in the best interest of his constitutional stance can be set aside, overruled, and changed by the incoming administration.

To not expect meddling of any kind by Russia in the affairs of the United States is to forget to be vigilant. You do not need the wisdom of Solomon to know that it is inevitable. Meddling should not be expected to be limited to elections only. What about the military, technology, and cyber ingenuity? What about in innovation and other areas of creativities? What about intelligence or technology shared by allies? Unless a bulletproof system is established and continues to be protected by the man or woman in the Oval Office, meddling in the affairs of the United States knows no bound and can happen when you least expected.

Those who would want the world to believe that they hate the United States are secretly praying that God would make it possible for them to come to the United States. No matter how you hate the United States, you cannot but be fascinated by its achievement, diversity, and composition in terms of talent and know-how.

That diversity and talent which is one of the bedrocks and core strength of the United States is going through an enormous and rigorous testing as a result of the reckless actions of the forty-fifth president of the United States—Donald J. Trump. American populace comprised of people who made every attempt to escape tyranny, persecution along with those seeking religious freedom. The United States became a safe haven for many citizens of different countries in their pursuit of happiness and a better life. It appears that the forty-fifth president of the United States, Donald J. Trump, is unaware of this important history of the United States.

The uncaring recklessness, divisive, and unprecedented attitude of Donald J. Trump are not only shocking but a tremendous deviation from the intent of the founding fathers. The speed at which the current president is trying to roll back most of what was done by his predecessor was no doubt reckless. The speed at which he was willing to criticize or even condemn minorities even when they are merely exercising their constitutional right to protest for rights is reckless. He is the source of his own inaccurate stories, which is due to his reckless way of trying to correct what could have been avoided. He is equally reckless in his desire to turn around and accuse the media of creating fake news when in reality, no one can keep up with his own multitude of fake news created due to the fact that he simply does not know how to be presidential.

What about his reckless way of criticizing with a never-ending attack on his own intelligence communities and even his own cabinet members as well as the FBI because of their unwillingness to recklessly rush into embracing his self-serving agenda but follow the rule of law! His number one goal was not to govern like any president before him but assemble people willing to follow him blindly in his effort to dismantle the structure that took years and a lot of efforts of many people regardless of their ethnic background and the color of their skin to build for the United States.

Why is it so important to accept everything about him and to not question his actions or intent? The answer is simple. It provides a way to cover his shady past, deed, and deals likely to expose the fact that the man in the Oval Office did not come as a friend of the people but an individual with a secret desire to rule with iron hands—a dictator waiting to unleash a new wave of discrimination, separatism, and inequality never before seen or experience in history. His like-minded friends and politicians in congress, senate, private sectors, and commerce are not afraid to jump to his defense and to help solidify his disdain for minorities along with his divisive agenda.

How much of his call for unity during his first state of the union address is due to the brilliant writing of his speechwriters in light of the mixed messages delivered to the American people? Before the address, news anchors were talking about his plan to unite the nation. While this was going on, one of his surrogates and stunt ally in congress, Republican congressman from California Devin Nunes, decided to make public the memo written by Nunes accusing the FBI of playing favoritism during the 2016 election even though his candidate won the election and now in the executive branch. Divisiveness and the desire to eliminate opposing views at all cost are no doubt the driving force behind the bully attitude and nonstop intimidation embarked upon by the man in the Oval Office and his like-minded supporters, friends, surrogates, and associates.

Before the Nunes memo could see the light of day, a news report revealed that the version Republicans voted to reveal was not the one Devin Nunes gave to the White House to be released. The original has been tampered with and changed. In addition to the two confusing versions is additional one new and completely different versions from one another. We now have three different versions of the same memo and that is not the end of the confusion. Why is creating chaos and turmoil the norm for this administration as opposed to the exception? It appears they genuinely hate transparency in the real sense of transparency but would rather dive into their selective transparency in the interest of chaotic and deviating outcome. They are just not interested in the truth and straightforwardness but a way to distract, confuse people, and in most cases outright lie about what is actually going on.

If you are caught in wrongdoing, admit nothing, confess nothing, offer no proof of your position, only point accusing fingers in the other direction and create "alternative fact" designed to cast doubt and confuse people further. As it turned out, the intent of the memo developed by Congressman Nunes was to accuse the Democrat as the one in collusion with Russia, make the FBI and other members of the intelligence communities look incompetent, corrupt, and demoralized. In other words, the goal was to make the United States look stupid in the eyes of the world.

Republicans and their evangelical friends would rather trade the integrity of the United States for a chance to solidify the platform of concealed hate, stay in control, and diplomatically and politically deny minorities a piece of the pie without having to worry about the divine law of God. After all, you have to be Norwegian to be granted citizenship, right? Nigerians should return to their huts, the entire continent of Africa is considered a shithole, and other nonwhite countries "are not sending their best" to the United States. Those seeking refuge should be sent back! Why should we care about those running from tyranny and persecution?

When women are abused, harassed, demeaned, and stepped on, the first thing is to believe the story of the accused and publicly show support for the accused. What about the victims of their abusive, harassment, barbaric, selfish, and wicked behaviors? If anything, make a liar out of them, nullify their stories and if public outcry is loud enough to not allow the story to go quietly into the night, you can then come back, break your silence after several days or weeks, only to say, "Of course I condemn domestic violence in every form." Very unfortunate that the president of the United States have to be dragged and chastised into apologizing like a three-year-old whose mom is saying, "I want you to say you are sorry to the lady" only to reluctantly turn around to say "I'm sorry!"

A rebuttal to the Nunes memo is prepared with the help of Adam Schiff, representative for California's twenty-eighth congressional district. What are the chances that President Trump would approve of the release of this rebuttal? This rebuttal is designed to show what the Democrats believe took place. In a truly transparent world, there is no reason not to release the memo.

The Democrat rebuttal is now ready and given to the president to be declassified and released to the general public. Somehow, the same president who promised to release the Nunes memo before reading it, so far, had refused to release the democrat memo unless it is redacted and resubmitted for consideration. All the Republicans including the speaker of the House and senate majority leader who were highly vocal concerning the need, desire, and eagerness to release Nunes memo because they believe in transparency had, so far, remained quiet and not interested in transparency this time around.

Call it hypocrisy, double standard, but the Trump people believe that any attempt to solidify the platform of hate is justified. Trump is at the forefront of a movement—the only movement of its kind since the coming together of the confederate masquerading their intent as nothing more than political agenda. But it has buyer-beware written all over it. So far, the evangelicals seem to like what is going on. They are not afraid to jump to the defense of Trump at any chance they get even though they did not do the same for Obama and did not do it for the Clintons. As far as they are concerned, God's mercy and forgiveness are for those sanctioned by the evangelicals. Agent of concealed hate is better and much more acceptable—just what the pastor ordered.

Investigation of Trump and his campaign in a possible collusion with Russia in the 2016 election, which propelled Trump to the citadel of power, has been expanded to include obstruction of justice and money laundering just to name a few. Nearly every member of his team is under the microscope. Some had been arrested and awaiting trial while some had pleaded guilty and awaiting sentencing. The investigation is closing in on the man himself, and his lawyers are asking him to refuse to testify. Those around him are saying that the advice given by Trump's lawyers not to testify is the best thing for him due to the fact that he, Trump, is "incapable of telling the truth." Really? This kind of defense speaks volume. To be "incapable of telling the truth" connotes that this individual had lived a life of lies to make him qualify as pathological liar who is "incapable of telling the truth," and this is the man at the apex of power in the United States.

It is ironic that the man elected to lead the most powerful nation on the planet is "incapable of telling the truth." No wonder his tweets and speeches are full of inaccurate information. However, he is quick to call other sources of information fake news.

What do those protecting Trump expect from public officials in the United States? Are they under the illusion that people are not supposed to lean in any way of interest to them regardless of their position, responsibility, and party affiliation? Did they forget that this is still "the land of the free and home of the brave"? Reality is that people are not robotic in nature. Expressing your view does not automatically translate into bias and unfair evaluation of the other side. It does not automatically translate into judging the other side negatively unless you are Trump supporters. None of them has ever said, "I think the president and the White House went too far in their reaction." They are not the kind of people who can beg to differ but still retain support and loyalty for Trump. They are not the type of people who can be fair and just at the same time. None of them seems to remember that Obama is no longer in the White House as the president of the United States. None of them seems to remember that there is a new sheriff in town and that he should stop blaming those before him and take responsibility for his action.

Adam Schiff's memo is finally released but redacted by Trump administration in conformity with their crooked and misleading version. However, it still managed to reveal the same truth.

HIDDEN AGENDA BEHIND "MAKE AMERICA GREAT AGAIN"

The United States came close to another unique type of recklessness when the man elected as the president inadvertently revealed what his desire to "make America great again" was all about. It became clear that he is not afraid to roll back the hand of time, thereby denying the tired, the poor, and the huddled masses yearning to breathe free and replace them with mainly Norwegians. There is no denying the fact that the call to "make America great again" is mainly to rid the United States of his minority population. The plan to isolate the United States coupled with the moral deficiency and wickedness going on, although exceptional, makes more sense when the president spoke explicitly but inadvertently about his secret desire.

The country of immigrants is unsuspectingly turning its back on immigrants. The country that have benefited immensely from the effort, knowledge, and talent of the "tired, the poor, and the huddled masses yearning to breathe free" is beginning to turn its back on those who have contributed a great deal to its greatness. The close-the-door approach carefully orchestrated by Donald J. Trump and his prejudiced team was actually designed to transform the "land of the free and the home of the brave."

What the Confederate cannot achieve because they were too bold, direct, too antiminorities is under review for a better, concealed, and sneaky strategies. If you think "make America great again" is nothing but a slogan, you could be in for a rude awakening. "Make America great again" is a project of passion designed to go further than the Confederate can ever imagine. Those who found this type of approach more acceptable, less imposing, less intrusive, and more defensible are standing by to lend a helping hand. They are not going out on a limb in support of what is explicit but to explain actions that seriously insults intelligence, which does not need explanation but to be accepted as the naked truth. There is no shortage of many mind readers who believe that they are ordained by God to help explain the rationale behind every action of the man responsible for the call to "make America great again."

Let us take a careful look at the call to "make America great again" by itself. When you look at actions taken on everything involving minorities by a man who is supposed to bring every ethnic group in the United States together, or words spoken in reference to minorities standing up for their right, or explicit deed of the president at every level, you simply cannot but conclude that to "make America great again" is a coded call to "make America white again." You do not need the wisdom of Solomon to agree with Matthew 12:34 that "out of the abundance of the heart the mouth speaks."

Africa—the land of extraordinary natural resources, treasures, gold, pearls of great prize all around the land, the birthplace of mankind, original homeland of the human family including the Norwegians and all the people of Europe—was rich in natural resources until those natural resources were forcefully extracted against the will of the inhabitants of Africa.

That ungodly extraction left a big hole now described as "shithole" by a man who benefited a great deal from those things forcefully removed from Africa. A man who likes to refer to himself as a "stable genius" but fails to realize that the hole left behind by the West is extremely difficult to cover up. Many inhabitants of Africa lost their lives trying to prevent the hole from being dug.

The hole filled with dead bodies, ocean of tears, pain, and heartaches—needless to say, the hole stinks to high heavens. It left many inhabitants of Africa destitute. We wouldn't have remembered it if not for the words of the man with nose big enough to still smell the unfriendly and deadly gas still coming out of that shitholes.

The most interesting part of the president's comment about Africa is that this is a hole that took many years to dig, and many countries in the Western world are solely responsible. It is a hole that many Africans would not mind to forget, like it never happened because of their forgiven spirit. A hole like this need a "shithole" eyes to see it and a "shithole" nose to sniff it out. Not only that, it usually takes a "shithole" mouth to speak so explicitly without the wisdom to think before such vile and vulgarity roll out of his "shithole" mouth.

When you become the president of the United States, you should know and realize that you are not a wrestling manager or boxing promoter. You are the leader of the most powerful nation on the planet. You are the man in the Oval Office, the one expected to be dignified and go beyond the call of duty to bring people together regardless of party affiliation. You are the one who should think before you speak and not speak before you think. You should know that you cannot engage in trash talk and wait for your surrogates to clean up the mess you created.

Why do you have to keep defending yourself as "the least racist person" all the time? The fact that you have to use the phrase "the least racist" person connotes (as my wife pointed out) that you are *racist* but not as much a racist as other racists. Why wouldn't you stay away from controversial and divisive rhetoric and focus on your agenda?

Two Republican senators who were both in the room jumped to the defense of this seventy-one-year-old man like he is too retarded to defend himself. Senators David Perdue of Georgia and Tom Cotton of Arkansas both came out saying, "I do not recall him saying anything derogatory to any individual or any person." The most shocking of their defense is that no one is accusing Donald J. Trump of using such derogatory words in reference to "any individual or any person" but to a continent—the birthplace of mankind.

When you look at most countries of the world, the dictatorial and totalitarian rule along with the control over what their citizens can do and enjoy, and the speed at which government, in the hand of the wrong man can wipe away freedom including freedom of religion and the press, you cannot but wonder! Constitution of most countries of the world can be changed or rewritten in the blink of an eye—nothing is carved in stone. Thank God that the constitution of the United States, like that of the city of God, remains the same even after the unsolicited intent to make America (United States) great again emerged; otherwise, Trump would have made the move to rewrite it to carry out his secret agenda.

United States is the only place where not much change is required; the only place where all you need to do is keep his bright light shining brighter and continue to improve her relationship with her allies and with God. It is the job of all God-fearing, freedom-loving, and caring citizens of the United States to prevent it from falling into the hands of an individual with secret agenda and concealed hate aimed at more than half of the human family.

A nation of "We the People" was about to become a nation of "us against them." The word *united* is about to be forever changed to *divided*. There was no reaching out to the rest of the world because the new desire is to get closer to dictators, civil right and human right abusers and totalitarian regimes around the world. United States is about to be divided against itself, and most people remain unsuspecting and unconcerned. By the same token, many did not want to see and believe the magnitude of disruption and division taking place from within.

The first strategy was to isolate the United States from his allies as well as from the rest of the world. This is like messing with the root of his military might. Somehow, the one behind this destructive change thinks that the United States is self-sufficient, therefore, do not need friendship of any other nation. He had forgotten that just like "no man is an island," so are countries—no country is an island. The military might of the United States lies in his ability to use the strength of her allies' intelligence to her advantage.

The second strategy was to give agent of division, within the United States, a new voice in the interest of political gain. This is not going to happen without given up attention to morality. The United States is great because of her "leaning on the everlasting arm." If sins are intentionally denied, buried, and treated as inconsequential, it will not make it go away but keep it alive and its consequences much stronger.

United States under Trump was preparing to stand against good; against the very foundation and against the source of her greatness. The intent to turn people against one another was more than just becoming the voice of hate group. The silent minority members of the privilege majority hard it loud and clear on the campaign trail that "I am your voice." They all saw that as a way to come out of the closet; as a result, they came out in record number demanding the impossible with the hope of meddling in the affairs of the Almighty.

The desire to come down on minorities like never before was out in the open. They were not afraid to demand what they think is theirs even though it's nothing but a false claim. One by one, they came out! What else could be scarier? Police officer explicitly cut loose in an unbridled manner when he inadvertently let out a new and silent code of conduct among his like-minded police officers when he loudly declared that "we only kill black people." Perhaps this is systemic! In light of the lightning rod reaction of every police officer ready to shoot any black person on the spot for whatever reason without paying attention to the core requirements of their training and the rule of law, and in light of their cookie-cutter defense mechanism of "He threatened my life," it is not too much to assume that this is something systemic and pandemic.

A white person can pull out a knife or even gun on a police officer only to post bail and go home to his family. However, a black man who has his hands up in obedience to the rule of law, is likely to end up in the mortuary. Body camera on any police officer is not a deterrent but a way to solidify false claim, and there is no shortage of jurors willing to go along.

A police officer who came out boldly saying to a motorist he routinely pulled over that "we only kill black people" did not draw any condemnation or reprimand—not from his precinct, not from any media outlet, not from the mayor of his city or the governor of his state, and definitely not from any lawmaker state or federal. This dangerous terroristic declaration that should have galvanized national attention disappeared into the night without response.

If that was a joke expected to be funny, it was a cruel joke. If that was his way of deescalating a situation, it was at a minimum extremely wicked, inhumane de-escalation tactics and at a maximum an expression of terroristic intent, which in fact is treason at its best and deserving the highest punishment the law can deliver. Instead, it was ignored and treated like a nonsignificant remark. The fact that there were no other police officers in his precinct or elsewhere around the country to speak publicly against this kind of bigotry and barbaric act of man's inhumanity to man proved that this is a known fact and silent code among many police officers expected to be executed without anyone publicly knowing that it exists. It was an action they believe can be effectively defended with a simple statement such as "I was afraid for my life." When you look at the alarming ready-made stamp of approval given by some judges in cases like this, it is not too much to conclude that we are living in a dangerous time.

How do you explain the action of a person running away from a police officer only to have his body riddled with bullets and killed instantly? What else could quickly erode public trust and confidence in people you are supposed to trust with your life regardless of the color of their skin or their ethnicity! We now know beyond the shadow of doubt that the duty related pledge "to protect and to serve" is scarily subjective. The nonchalant attitude and lack of response from other law enforcement officers shows that this type of outburst, "We only kill black people," is explicitly and absolutely true.

What can prompt the arrest and prosecution of the most hardened white criminal can quickly escalate to the killing of a black family man who was perhaps under the impression that he was behind on his child support payment, therefore running to avoid arrest only to have his existence come to abrupt end in the hand of a police officer looking for black people to kill. We are indeed living in a dangerous time, and this simple fact can never be over emphasized.

To say that hate is everywhere is an understatement. The hope of escaping tyranny, oppression, religious persecution, and injustice is now coming face-to-face with a formidable and bigger challenge. A carefully orchestrated plan in the hand of unsuspectingly sneaky tyrants is about to test the foundation on which the United States is built.

George Washington was a believer in freedom. Thomas Jefferson was not afraid to declare that "all men are created equal." Abraham Lincoln was bent on destroying hate and segregation. He stuck his neck out in the pursuit of one truly United States of America. Against all opposition and against all odds, he stood boldly and gave Emancipation Proclamation to all of God's children. However, Donald J. Trump and his white nationalists together with other extremists are on a different mission—a mission to help resurrect, preserve, and nurture hate and division like never before. The main problem is that the general public is, no doubt, gullible.

What we are experiencing is more than political differences, ideology, or simply different strategies to win votes and solidify support. This is about hidden agenda rooted and grounded in something deeper than just blank rhetoric and excusable behaviors people thought was coming from an inexperienced individual who found himself at the apex of power. "Draining the swamp" carries something more sinister, something more diabolical, something more divisive, and completely against the rebuilding of the human family than anything we have ever seen in history.

If you think he was on a mission to preserve offensive monument and that his speech concerning "good people on both sides" was referring to any of those controversial historical monuments, you are simply following blindly. As a matter of fact, that's one of the strangest explanations ever developed to defend a seventy-one-year-old erratic and pathological liar with unrepentant and divisive mind who is not afraid to offend anyone.

The fact that many are willing to make excuses for this grown man is frighteningly appalling. Those who like to defend him are doing it like as if to say that "he is only a twelve-year-old. What do you expect?" The fact of the matter is that he is not a twelve-year old, he is not an inexperienced politician, and he is not naïve. He is completely aware of his actions and the fact that he genuinely believes that he is "the only one who can fix it."

Do not forget that the initial message of Adolf Hitler was well received among his like-minded people who were not afraid to defend him at every level. By the time they all realized that his rhetoric was more than just a public stand for nationalistic interest, it was too late. Evil descended upon the entire nation of Germany like they had never seen before and delivered paralyzing chill and intimidation on a scale never delivered in human history.

It is obvious that economic prosperity (job growth and steady stock market growth on Wall Street) of 2017 started during the Obama administration continues! The campaign to stop jobs from going to Mexico has not produce expected result. Coal miners are yet to see what was promised to them; Chinese ambition to replace the United States as the world's leading economic power is getting stronger each day and each week. United States of America continues to turn his back on his allies. When it comes to North Korea, what the Secretary of State is supposed to do was almost outsource to Russia when Mr. Putin offered to mediate.

The entire so-called tax relief is built on speculation that corporate profit would, in the end, lead to jobs and more jobs despite the possible increase in the deficit. The jury is out on that. Presidential tweets—good or bad but mostly bad and could have been avoided—are difficult to control because of the president's urge and desire to fight back. He is a "counterpuncher" regardless of whether he is the president of the most powerful country on the planet.

This is the time to ask some probing questions such as, what is this uncanny fascination of Donald J. Trump with dictatorship, iron-clad and ruthless grip on power all about? Why is it so difficult to convince, work with, and win the support of opponents including supporters who merely disagree with a specific action? Why is it so easy to attack them at every tweet and at every opportunity? Is this really the man who wrote *The Art of the Deal*?

Don't let anyone fool you, the "good people on both sides" comment in response to Charlottesville was referring to those physically present there. He was simply trying to legitimize and humanize hate and hate group as well as their mission—pure and simple. What is wrong is wrong. There is no other way to paint the picture of hate. Those who are morally deficient needs to hear the fact!

Hate in religion, in politics, in business, in government, and in every facet of human interaction must be identified, called out, and dealt with without fear and without trying to hide behind unmindful and divisive rhetoric and tweets. The hope of defeating hate is in the hand of those who are not afraid to stand up for what is right. It is in the hand of those not afraid to take a high and unyielding moral ground. Jews are not the enemy; black people are not the enemy; Hispanics, Asians, Native Americans or any member of the minority group are not the enemy.

Those who are making unreasonable demand of "we want our country back" or "we want our streets back" need to understand in the words of John Donne that "no man is an island entire of itself; every man is a piece of the continent, a part of the main." No country in the world can completely claim that they belong to one people, one culture, and one language any more than they can claim that the world belongs to them only. United States of America is no exception. What was true yesterday cannot be held as true today. Our dependence on one another in every aspect of life speaks volume.

It is not uncommon nowadays to see people of another culture and language speaking a different language fluently. You can never complete your day without products made in other countries or food once exclusive to a specific people and culture on the dining table of those who are not from that ethnic group and culture. Not only that, you would be surprised to see other people making food or product that used to be the signature food and product of a specific country and culture in another and completely different country and culture better than where it originated from. The line of originality is not only becoming blurrier and wearing thin, it is beginning to disappear. The unity of ethnicities is inevitable regardless of further attempt to divide and segregate.

Love cannot be localized and cannot be legislated. It has never been and cannot be. The idea that a citizen of a specific country must fall in love and marry one another exclusively is as unrealistic as it is ungodly and against human desire and happiness. It is certainly restrictive and no doubt laughable and undermines the fact that "opposite attracts."

The fact that we are connected through bloodline makes it difficult to continue this cankerworm rat race of superiority. Let members of hate groups check their DNA, and they would discover that the blood that runs through their veins completely disagrees with their dangerous claim of superiority. Once the truth is discovered, they might drop their unsubstantiated claim like a bad habit or die defending what is not realistic and true.

Children of light cannot and must not stoop down to the level of retaliating hate with hate or blow with blow. We are better than that. The need for higher moral ground necessitates that we do not subscribe to violence and hate. The interconnected aspect of humanity dictates that we respect one another, listen to the voice of the oppressed, and never stop to continue to fight for and defend those who cannot fight for or defend themselves. This land belongs to all of us. The United States of America is still the land of "We the people."

> "This Land is your land; this land is my land. From
> California to the New York island. From the
> Redwood Forest, to the gulf stream waters This
> Land was made for you and me."

WHO IS DONALD J. TRUMP?

Intent to divide was never hidden nor a mystery! Disdain for any group of minorities along with innate misconception due to his upbringing but not hereditary was not designed to surprise anyone. Trump never tried to pretend and never tried to hide his intolerance for minorities who are, as he perceived it, on lawless ride and on handouts. Concealed resentment transformed into concealed hate, which was difficult for him to get rid of but remains indelible in his understanding and acceptance of minorities. Trump was never a lone wolf struggling to understand why many of the so-called minorities are getting free ride. Without any effort to understand, Trump stepped forward as the voice of those who think they are being taking advantage of.

Trump, like a spoiled child, grew up with silver spoon in his mouth. His father was a successful real estate mogul. Trump went to one of the best schools in the United States only to become, by his own design and by his own doing, such a mediocre but privileged student who scaled through on family name and success. He did not and still does not like to read. He always like to read titles or headline to imagine the story and then conclude. He has an incredibly short attention span with inexplicable inability to stay focused and remain focused without getting bored and quickly looking for something else to do. He hates to search for better and credible information, hence the tendency to misunderstand, thereby assume opposite to exact meaning or intended meaning—example: global warming. He is not a deep thinker. He does not believe in opinion of others but his. His mind has a way of deceiving him and getting him into believing that whatever he thinks and believe is authentic.

"I learned this from my father" is not one of those things you will ever hear from Trump. No opinion can ever come close or superior to his! He is not big at quoting anyone; that would be shifting focus by giving credit to others. Trump believe he is "all knowing" even if the knowledge he possessed is superbly inferior with no basis in fact. He can never do wrong.

Don't forget, he is "kind of smart and a stable genius." "Kind of smart" is like not smart at all. How many geniuses do you know going around and bragging about being a genius? That by itself carries such an unbelievable negative connotation. If you believe that the ability to label and call others derogatory names until you make people hate them in order to win election means you are a genius, think again. That's like a bully calling a beautiful girl "ugly" until the girl begins to believe it, thereby hating herself and does the unthinkable—that is far from being a genius. That is insensitive, cruel, wicked and evil.

Despite his out-of-this-world arrogant and beyond-reproach attitude, he came out of school into an established life. When he expressed interest in starting his own business, he was lucky to receive a one-million-dollar support from his father. He did not know what it is to submit a truckload of resumes just to land an entry-level job you hate and walk your way up the ladder of success by hanging out with people you would have loved to avoid. He was placed on the ladder with no questions asked. He did not know or understand prejudice, discrimination, or what it means to prove who you are or what you know. He was born into opportunities. One of the questions that kept bugging his mind includes why does the federal government have to step in to help the disadvantaged including the so-called minorities?

He never had the desire, dream, or the passion to dream of helping the deprived. If anything, there was no inner drive to walk across the aisle and offer a glass of water to the shut-ins. Trump never knew what helping others really mean. Why should anyone care about the less fortunate? That part of him was never developed, hence the arrogant person he grew up to be who thinks he deserve loyalty and gratitude from others. He saw himself, earlier on, as self-made—an individual with no reason to care or be concerned about what most people would consider misfortune of others.

Christianity did not make it any easier for him to see why he should "give a glass of water to the least of these." Identifying with the unfortunate was not in him. He was too far removed from reality and too far removed from humanity.

In case you are wondering how he managed to hire and work with some minorities, the answers are twofold. Number one, affirmative action did not make it any easier for him to avoid minorities completely. However, if the government is making it a little difficult to avoid minorities, thereby ignoring and staying away from them, why not look for a way to get to the citadel of power to help initiate permanent change? One of two options of this subsection became extremely appealing to him. The first was to come into government as an authoritarian, a dictator if possible. How is that really possible in the land of "We the People?" For this reason, he developed exclusive and unyielding fascination to the philosophy, life, and rule of dictators, those who like to rule their country with iron hand all around the world. The second subsection was to turn against minorities from within using every hate group you can think of to attack minorities. He failed to realize that God Himself was at the very foundation of this country named "the United States." Not only that, he did not realize that "behind the dim unknown, God is standing in the shadow, keeping watch above His own."

As for the second reason why Trump hired and worked with minorities, if you do not have a believable voice likely to drown out Trump, you are bound to enjoy a conspicuous place under his shadow. If you are willing to let him gloat at your expense and you are highly unlikely to resist, you are bound to enjoy being seeing with him. He is under the illusion that your so-called success and glory will be far better under his umbrella.

The separatists, supremacists, segregationists, Alt-rights, neo-Nazis, and many others like them are already too frustrated and helpless in their attempt to further isolate all minorities until Trump showed up saying, "I am your voice." Trump's disdain for, and resentment of, minorities had already gone deeper than what any of the groups mentioned in this paragraph had intended. Trump already developed unrepentant fascination into creating a never-before-seen changes not only in the United States but all around the world. What he would like to implement in the United States was intercepted by the voice of opposing views based on the irrational speed of his yet to be fully revealed plan.

He won the election. He became the leader of the Free World. His first agenda was to change whatever can be changed right away most especially any achievement of his immediate predecessor who happened to be member of the same minority group. "Whatsoever is good" change them. "Whatsoever is of a good report" that can help people succeed in life, change them also. Let us create our own stories designed to make everything believable and if any journalist opposes, label the journalist and his or her organization as "fake news" outlet.

Another side of Trump most people do not often see is the fact that if he can get away with paying as little as possible for quality work, you can be rest assured that your name will be carved in his friendship book of honor. He enjoys exploring the possibility of paying as little as possible to get any job done. If Trump was so pro–"made in the United States," why is it so difficult to have any of his brands proudly and truthfully enjoy the label of "made in the USA"?

The most ironic part of Trump is the fact that when it comes to Trump everybody is a mind reader. They are not afraid to defend him blindly and excuse him to no end. "The president did not mean it that way" or "You misunderstood him." They had forgotten that this is a seventy-one-year-old man who is not afraid to speak his mind. Every time one of his surrogates is asked about what Trump said, they all seem to know how to eloquently defend him. However, within the same day or in some case, the same hour, Trump is going to come out, via tweet or unbridled and raw speech or response to questioning, and confirm, explicitly, what he said and not afraid to stir up controversy.

Nearly everyone around Trump refused to believe that Trump loves attention and likes to magnify self-glorification, and if none is awarded, he is not afraid to create one and put it out there even if it is fake and completely fabricated. One of his common saying is that "people are telling me this is the 'best' in the history of this country." Another one is that "we have achieved more within a short period of time than any of my predecessors." Everything about Trump is either the best or "huge." He simply does not like it when another member of the human family receives more accolades, more recognition, and more attention than him, hence the beef with an American icon such as Senator John McCain or the first

African American duly elected president of the United States of America and others like them.

How is it possible for President Obama, a minority, whose father is from Kenya and his mom an American citizen, managed to gain admission into an Ivy League, he came out and climbed the ladder of success within a short period? What federal government program allowed him to be this successful so fast? What about those football players who became rich and famous just by playing spot?

When Trump looks at the success of any minority person, it is difficult for him to see struggle, perseverance, and determination. He sees people who took a shortcut to success. Trump was never given the chance to compete; he did not know what it means to struggle and proof himself! He had no idea what role the determination to succeed plays in what people do in spite of unimaginable obstacles and against all odds!

What is the fascination with asking all his cabinet members to continually sing his praises and for a never-ending loyalty? You have to publicly thank him, worship and adore him for allowing you to serve to remain on his good side. His vice president will never stop praising him like he is some kind of deity. Mike Pence, who is supposed to be a Christian, simply do not know where gratitude and appreciation ends and worshiping begins. How can you sit there praising—day in, day out—a guy who sits boldly with his arms folded looking like a statute while soaking in every praise, every adoration, every public worship, and on top of it all, smiling? I guess part of the vice president's job requirements is to continually kiss the ground Donald J. Trump walks on every five minutes of his time in Washington or perhaps for the rest of natural life. I wonder how many times he has to devote to praising God if he is so immersed in worshiping Trump every chance he gets. As for Trump himself, how many times has he ever said, "Thank you, Lord God Almighty, for allowing me to serve."

The entire Republican leadership had to shower him with phrase such as "your exquisite leadership," "the best leader in the history of the United States," "your strong leadership," "friend of the deprived," "concerned leader," and more. No wonder one of the ads for Trump in December of 2017 was a "thank you" advertisement with a bunch of his supporters saying "thank you" endlessly.

You just have to wonder if the Republican party is still the party claiming to be more evangelical than any other parties in the history of politics. What is going on with the party of Abraham Lincoln? Are we witnessing a new political blindness and erosion of morality on a scale never before experienced in history? Flesh and blood (mortal) is now elevated to the level of God Almighty (immortal) and worship as such most especially by the people who are supposed to know better!

Trump does not know how to win anyone's love or admiration in any way, a man who cannot walk across political aisle to convince those on the other side to see his point of view, a man who cannot let a simple disagreement go without seriously attacking those who disagreed without going on his popular platform, Twitter. If you believe that Trump wrote *The Art of the Deal,* brace yourself. It is evident from his action as the president that he did not! It was written for him. Trump could have done better with "The Art of Attack" or "The Art of Intimidation," "The Art of Denial," "The Art of Distraction" or better yet, "The Art of Using Twitter to Create Division." Trump grew into an unrepentant and monumental privileges with no one to revere or appreciate, hence his arrogant persona.

Inconsistencies in the interest of financial gain are not uncommon to Trump. He is a man who would say or do anything for a handsome financial reward. Trump, whose heritage was no doubt German, denies that for years in his effort to sell apartments to Jewish families in New York.

In a tweet responding to Elizabeth Warren, senior senator from Massachusetts as having native of American heritage, Donald Trump Jr. wrote the following:

> "Really! Interesting. Out of curiosity, what would you call pretending to be something you are not for financial gain? Other than fraud of course . . ."

If that was true, what would you call Donald J. Trump himself? In his so-called autobiography, *The Art of the Deal,* Trump talked about his grandfather as Swedish in an attempt to intentionally deviate from his German root. On several occasions, he denied the fact that his father is a German in the interest of financial gain. In the words of Trump Jr., "What would you call pretending to be something you are not for financial gain? Other than fraud of course?"

Trump had enjoyed the glare of convenience under the shadow of inherited wealth and not as an innovator or even entrepreneur. He had managed to convince lenders and investors not to take action likely to tip him over most especially when his vulnerability as a novice businessman was about to be exposed. He had managed to protect anything likely to expose his true worth or his incompetent side or the crooked ways in which he operates. Some of what could have exposed him, such as his tax returns and other financial blueprint including how he managed to intimidate employees and avoid paying for job well done, are protected and guarded like treasure of a great price.

He is very good at creating his own reality in the face of his alternative truth, which by itself is a lie carefully orchestrated to look like the truth. This has always been a consistent strategy of Trump designed to shift focus and attention away from him to somebody or perhaps something else. No one could be more crooked than Donald J. Trump!

Alternative truth, alternative fact, distractions, and manipulation have always been part of Trump's brand. The fact that he is so good at twisting the facts in favor of creating doubt, thereby shifting focus by making people go "Maybe he was right" had given his crooked way a seemingly logical platform! By the same token, the fact that this had gone on for so many years makes it more pathological and odder than anything! All these are designed to insult intelligence. If you think Trump is going to change or repent, it is a little too late for that.

Trump has always been his own man, his own source of truth expected to be absolute truth. He does not have appetite or patience for any opinion or input in his affairs that tend to negate his belief or knowledge. He does not understand what constructive criticism means. He is in a business not subject to intensive government rules and regulations and not subject to the dictate of any board of directors or shareholders but his own instinct and his cronies' agreement. Trump Organization, which some people believe made him qualified as an experienced businessman, is just an elaborate, and high profiled mom-and-pop business located on a prestigious street and rich municipality in New York—Manhattan.

To operate like Trump, you don't have to do anything to attract clients other than to make the business look glamorous, high class, and give yourself a superrich outlook that may or may not be rooted in truth plus intimidating persona and above-reproach attitude. Deeper business knowledge is not required, and scientific business strategies necessary for greater success is not necessary. Why is it so difficult to produce tax return to justify net worth, most especially when others running for the same public office are very forthcoming in the production of the same?

You do not have to be a genius to grow a business-like Trump's. All you need are dependable number of assistants and lieutenants not interested in questioning your authority and your truthfulness but continue to follow you every step of the way. Advertisement and promotions are good but optional. The true spirit of competition is not there as long as you are well connected. Besides conforming to standard employment requirements, state ordinances, and county requirements, there is basically nothing that can threaten the very existence of the business. To call an individual like Trump an experienced business man is subject to interpretation. To be so arrogant to have a book entitled *The Art of the Deal* insults intelligence unless it is presented as purely fictional and subjective.

Trump's ideology and philosophy including approach to sins, although very simple and straightforward, deserve to be highlighted! Morality is on a downward spiral; divine intervention is being intentionally ignored and marginalized by political influence. Everything Christ demanded of us is being regarded as "liberal agenda." Some evangelicals are stepping forward with intent to take over the role of the Almighty. Praying and believing in God to change things are being replaced by political representation and hands on in Washington. They are not afraid to proclaim that they are now ordained with the power to not only reclassify sin but also the power to forgive whatever is considered sinful and set aside any behavior they view or see differently.

There is a large segment of the evangelicals who believe that nothing can be done without appealing to a president who does not understand what following in the steps of Christ means or who is willing to acknowledge the presence of God. An individual with extraordinary big ego who craves adoration and a permanent place in the limelight—a person who want to be first and see whatever he does as either "the best ever" or "the first in history." You can never stop praising him and still remain in his favored circle or be counted worthy by him!

The branch of evangelicals supporting him couldn't care less about his antagonistic attitude and his intentional disregard for the purpose or the reason Christ died for the sins of many. His out-of-this-world crusade of division among the people of God along with an unprecedented and un-Christian cultural war instigated by him was indeed a melodious music to the ears of his evangelical friends.

The branch of evangelicals he attracted are too busy looking for what they considered as the right political ideology, robotic, and rubber-stamp judges on the Supreme Court bench to help solidify conservative agenda. To this group of people, prayers cannot change anything anymore; they have to physically make changes without allowing the Almighty to rule in the affairs of men.

It is more important to have a Conservative appointed to the Supreme Court than to ask the president to stop setting people against one another or stop the cultural war started by him. If your sins are exposed, the man they support believe you should deny it and do not acknowledge it even if proven. As for any news outlet broadcasting the exposed, it's okay to go ahead and label them as fake news. Do not admit anything and do not confess them to God or to anyone.

They are aware of the fact that once their sins are confessed to God, they cannot come out and declare publicly that it never happened. That by itself is worse than lying under oath. The Bible says, "It is a fearful thing to fall into the hands of the living God" (Hebrew 10:31). The only thing to do is deny, deny, and deny. If any news outlet keeps bringing them up, hit the news outlet as "fake news" over and again until you can make it stick.

If the public is very loud, insist that you did not do any of those things. Go ahead and shame those courageous enough to come forth. It is okay to insist on denial without presenting proof of any kind or any evidence to the contrary. Never mind what the Bible says in the book of 2 Chronicles 7:14, "If my people, who are called by my name, will humble themselves and pray and seek my face and turn from their wicked ways, then I will hear from heaven, and I will forgive their sin and will heal their land." What matters is to have Conservative Supreme Court judges and a Republican in the White House. Forget about "obedience is better than sacrifice." In this day and age, sacrifice is actually better than obedience. The evangelicals' rule in the affairs of men! They are not concerned about the gospel. They are all about politics pure and simple.

Some evangelicals believe that they, and not God, are ordained with the power to forgive sins, regulate morality, and handpick those they believe are righteous enough to lead. You think they would let their vote speak for them along with the power of prayer, thereby letting God be God and let politicians be politicians without trying to speak explicitly as to who is fit to serve and who is not!

They are not leery rushing to the White House to lay hands on the man who once said he will not confess sin or ask God or any man for forgiveness. His followers too will not admit wrongdoing, and they are not afraid to point out through tweeting or even hold press conferences and rallies to expose the sins of others. As for Trump, the general practice is to not admit wrongdoing and consistently and relentlessly insist that what was exposed are from fake news sources.

If the video of Trump's sin along with his bragging is aired all over for the world to see and a lot of women talked openly about what Trump did to them, his supporters are ready to treat his bragging as "locker-room" talk and label his accusers as liars. If Trump refused to admit, why should Roy Moore or anyone with ties to Trump admit to wrongdoing? Al Franken admitted to what he was accused of, confessed, and asked his accuser(s) for forgiveness. For the so-called evangelicals as well as those who lives in the so-called Bible Belt, political affiliation is what matters.

Some of these evangelicals believe that God is involved in favoritism. They believe that God can forgive Trump even if he did not explicitly ask God for forgiveness but will not forgive Hillary Clinton who was not arrogant to ask for forgiveness.

Initial reaction of some of Trump supporters is that "we did not vote for a church pastor." Don't we all know that! However, they had forgotten that the Bible is not written for church pastors but for children of God as well as "whosoever will." Confession of sin and repentance are expected of everyone to initiate divine forgiveness, acceptance, and anointing regardless of your status. If you are too arrogant and proud to obey God, it does not matter your political affiliation or who you think you are; you would soon discover that the Most High rules in the kingdom of men.

The system that helped propelled Trump to the top—the man Senator Lindsey Graham in 2016 describes as a "kook, crazy and unfit for the highest office in the land,"—that system clearly deserves a revamp.

United States is supposed to be the torchbearer of Democracy with the real government of the people, by the people, and for the people without any reason to doubt. Instead, Democracy in the United States has become government of the evangelicals and the privileged few who are not afraid to walk away from the very foundation of this great nation.

Whoever introduced the electoral college in the United States inadvertently introduced a way to set aside the will of the people, thereby replacing it with the will of the chosen few. Electoral college is designed to undermine Democracy from within and overrule the will of the people without twisting arms. It is not better than the party elite stepping out to set aside result of an election and appoint the person of interest to them.

The United States should not be divided by red and blue or anything; unfortunately, it is. The land of "We the People" should not be divided by the label of conservative and liberal; unfortunately, it is. There is no shortage of nations willing to take advantage of the implosion taking place from within. United States is about to deviate from the very foundation responsible for its greatness, and those who are supposed to be concerned are too busy following Donald J. Trump blindly.

Trump was too naïve and grossly disconnected from reality to lead a nation as powerful as the United States. Ironically, he became the president, and Republican Party lost the right to claim family value. Morality is on life support, and the voice of moral majority is silenced in favor of party loyalty. This is not a family business and certainly not expected to be a testing ground for arrogant and uninformed ignorant mind who is too proud and too polarized to see, understand, and do what it takes to help this nation remain as a dominant factor in economic growth, military might, and technological development.

Could it be that the problem with North Korea is not only the intent to develop nuclear weapon per se but to distract the United States, keep them focused on something as equally significant as the desire to keep up with fast changes created by Trump and worth focusing on while many countries are lining up to take advantage of the distraction. It may look like those countries are trying to help, but try not to forget that "the enemy of my enemy is my friend" is very much a popular modus operandi around the world.

UNYIELDING SPIRIT OF FRIENDS OF THE HUMAN FAMILY

The intent to scare, stop, or even kill a messenger of goodwill in hopes of ending the message he or she is inspired to deliver is as old as the history of man. There are so many people who genuinely hate the truth for various reasons. Greed-induced hate as well as prejudice built on selfish intent can, no doubt, blind the visions of men. They couldn't care less about humanity and about divine voice. If anything, they are not afraid to present their own version of the type of interactions approved by God. Their diabolical minds simply love darkness more than anything else but prefer to project godliness and everything, they think, beneficial to mankind.

One thing unknown to this greedy group of people who simply love to rub others of their worldly possessions is that there is a great deal of people who hate their dark and deceiving appearance as well as their self-righteous godliness. Regardless of any attempt to silence the dissenting voice (at least, that's what they call those who are bold and courageous enough to stand for what they believe in), God's will shall be done.

Prior to the reemergence of hate, something spectacular happened. A new way to make maximum negative and humiliating impact came to light. Many laws passed to divide humanity along color line and discriminate in ways pleasing to that agent of hate and division. They managed to lay the foundation for brutality (against Africans and those with traces of African in their blood) unimaginable through series of unjust and inhumane laws.

Their intent to hide behind religion to make their actions look like they were approved by God can be seen from a distance by any God-fearing and God-loving individual who is not afraid to stand for what is right.

In 1849, Henry David Thoreau wrote his essay on civil disobedience, which later became the bedrock of the civil rights movement. At the time when many children of darkness were busy looking for a way to change the course of history, many children of light simply refused to stand idly by and do nothing or say nothing. One of those who decided to do something was Henry David Thoreau (1817–1862). As reported by Richard J. Schneider in his article on "Thoreau's Life" published in the Thoreau Society: "Thoreau was an ardent and outspoken abolitionist, serving as a conductor on the Underground Railroad to help escaped slaves make their way to Canada. He wrote strongly worded attacks on the Fugitive Slave Law ('Slavery in Massachusetts') and on the execution of John Brown." In 1846, his unyielding spirit finally led to the writing of his popular essay on civil disobedience. Those epic instruments written in favor of alternative action against the evil intent of unjust laws paved the way for nonviolent resistance.

Figure 6. Henry D. Thoreau

Henry Thoreau did the best he could before he answered the last call. A new president by the name of Abraham Lincoln won the election and found himself wrestling with what to do about those who are left behind, those who are about to be pushed into the background and possibly facing annihilation in the hand of unspeakable brutality of hate. Part of his agenda includes the desire to no longer deny Africans the promise of

America. He was bent on making sure these segments of the population were not left behind. He stood to answer the call of conscience despite the dissenting voices at home and abroad.

Figure 7. Abraham Lincoln

As reported by the Civil War Trust, Abraham Lincoln genuinely struggled with how best to approach the declaration of one of his major achievements—Emancipation Proclamation. He issued preliminary version before the real deal. "Abraham Lincoln issued the preliminary Emancipation Proclamation on September 22nd, 1862. It stipulated that if the Southern states did not cease their rebellion by January 1st, 1863, then Proclamation would go into effect. When the Confederacy did not yield, Lincoln issued the final Emancipation Proclamation on January 1st, 1863." Despite the display of violence by the Confederacy, the president did not relent in his effort to move forward with Emancipation Proclamation.

There was a high mountain of oppositions to the emancipation proclamation at home and abroad. Many people within the military and other branches of government including political parties did not hide their opposition to Emancipation Proclamation. General John McClernand, argued "that the Emancipation Proclamation would impede chances of peace."

As reported by the World Socialist Web Site, the British ruling circles colluded with the confederacy and the "Southern operatives to blame the Union and Abraham Lincoln for the serious economic suffering caused by war." They did not hide their opposition to Emancipation Proclamation. Despite the opposition, about "as many as 3,000 workers packed into St. James' Hall in London" in support of President Lincoln "administration for the Emancipation Proclamation. The gathering was one of the most outstanding episodes of British working-class opposition to the Confederacy and slavery during the US Civil War (1861–1865)."

Lincoln's unyielding "intent to issue the final document on January 1, 1863, effectively prevented England, which had abolished slavery in its own territories, from stepping into the United States conflict."

In spite of all those unexpected opposition, those willing to be coworkers with God did not relent. Their persistent effort changed the cause of history. Prior to independence, a lot of laws and ordinances passed in the United States. They were deliberately and intentionally designed to limit interactions, segregate people, no doubt discriminate and dehumanize.

The Confederacy was adamant and unrepentant. They found a worthy ally—Britain as well as the Church of England and the Queen including France did not hide their opposition to Emancipation Proclamation. Ironic, isn't it? To see that an institution established to create a trustworthy bridge between God and man, an institution expected to be the conscience of the world, was completely highjacked and used as political and selfish tools in the destruction of those members of the same human family created in the image of the Most High God. Not only was that ministers (those ordained as servants of God) not allowed by the Church of England to serve the living God. They became servants of two masters, but the voice of the earthly master was more forceful to resist. Their role was reduced to that of a rubber stamp for the British government and the Queen. It didn't matter if the children of God were in pain, mental anguish, and suffering bodily harm in the hand of the greedy few. To them, it was better to look the other way than to stand for what is right in obedience to what the Bible says.

However, President Lincoln was determined. As reported by Steve Jones in ThoughtCo, "At his inauguration on March 4, 1861, Lincoln reiterated his stance. He had no intention to address slavery where it presently existed, but he *did* intend to preserve the Union. If the southern states wanted war, he would give it to them." This really proved that no one can silence the voice of truth. Threat of whatever would energize more than intimidate. In the words of William Shakespeare, "Cowards die many times before their death." Only a brave heart can stand determined.

Circumstances prompted Mohandas Karamchand Gandhi to take a stand. With no intention to miss a great opportunity, he quickly became inspired to wage spiritual warfare, built on the principle of nonviolence through civil disobedience, in favor of the liberation and independence of India and Pakistan. It did not stop there; the impact of the essay of Henry Thoreau on the mission of Gandhi along with extremely ambitious effort inspired Dr. Martin Luther King Jr. to stand for nonviolent resistance. Rebellion against hate is nothing new. Focusing on intimidating tactics will eventually help no one but create one gigantic society full of evil. Those who hate the ugliness of hate and simply love the beauty and the ever-glowing brightness of love have seen and experienced something bigger than any individual within the human family. As a result, they are not willing to look the other way and allow hate and evil to have the last say in the history of man.

Figure 8. Mohandas K Gandhi

Just like Gandhi, a young minister by the name of Martin Luther King Jr., who just assumed the role he was ordained to assume, received a new calling. This one was bigger than him and completely unexpected. However, saying no was not an option. He was ready and took to the podium of that historic Baptist church in Montgomery, Alabama, with such an unexpected boldness and divine inspiration and oratory beyond his years. His message came with such firmness and undeniable determination to echo the sentiment of fellow brothers and sisters who are suffering. The young minister stood without fear, with the hope of an entire ethnic group (not just in the United States but all over the world) on his shoulder. This was not about him; this was about the people he was called to serve. When he got up and boldly declared as firmly as possible that "we are tired now," the sound of the roaring response confirmed that he was speaking for the overwhelming majority of American. Although he did the best he could, but there is still more to be done.

What happened in Montgomery, Alabama, provided an unprecedented connection to all the sufferings of the past and put them all on the platform of things to address. Things were quickly connected, and those whose voice was once silenced and pushed into oblivion could no longer remain silent.

To say that many upright citizens and children of light were unaware of the premise and the thought behind the development of that historic presidential action, signed about one hundred years earlier, known as the Emancipation Proclamation, was unfathomable. The suffering did not end, discrimination did not end, and being treated as second-class citizens did not end. Unimaginable brutality and polarization in the country went on even after President Lincoln left office! America defaulted on many of the provisions of Emancipation Proclamation.

Segregation brought about by so many English laws passed in the 1700s was never reversed or erased. The future was exceedingly dark and dreary for many Africans. There was a new attack initiated. This new attack was not about depriving them of what was available to them prior to the 1700; among them is freedom to enjoy life like any other ethnic group as well as freedom to love and fall in love with anyone. The new attack was to drag those Africans who came to this country as explorers including those who came out of their own free will into slavery—something that was not meant for them. Those free men and women who did not come to this country as slaves were about to be rounded up and forever get entangled in slavery. It sickened many children of God to see many people of African descent as well as some other minorities losing their freedom in record numbers.

Many Africans who were already in the Americas and most especially in the United States were permanently denied their citizenship rights and ridiculed by the privileged few. No one was there to stand for them or fight for them. The forces of evil were everywhere, and the intent to inflict maximum pain on a scale never before seen was carefully planned and supported by kings, queens, and their kingdoms. The Confederacy felt invincible and above the law.

Greed-induced hate got hold of those who thought they were ordained by God to take what is not rightfully theirs and even kill for it. The most ironic part of this was the fact that the Church of England was dragged into this selfish mission, thereby bring blemish and unspeakable stain on the church. Greed did not allow them to want to share and enjoy this planet with any other ethnic group. They refused the call to exist side by side with anyone with African blood in them.

How free people ended up in slavery defies logic. They came here as free men and women. The desire to exercise their right to own properties— land as well as slaves of another ethnic group—and even fall in love with anyone led to many laws designed to restrict, punish them, and forever tarnish and dehumanize them. Their fight for equality fell on deaf ears, and kingdoms, institutions, and many individuals rose against them all in the effort to shame them and drown their noble quest for equality. It did not look like it was going to be an easy task, but as recited by Gloria Gaither in one of many songs by the Gaithers:

God has always had a people . . .

Many a foolish conqueror has made the mistake of thinking that because he had forced the church of Jesus Christ out of sight, he had stilled its voice and snuffed out its life. But God has always had a people! The powerful current of a rushing river is not diminished because it is forced to flow underground; the purest water is the stream that bursts crystal clear into the sunlight after it has forced its way through solid rock! But God has always had a people, men who could not be bought and women who were beyond purchase. God has always had a people!"

ANTONYM OF HATE: ANTITHETICAL

No doubt, hate came into this world for one important mission and that is "to steal, to kill, and to destroy." Hate set the human family against one another through greed-induced hate. Hate held us at gunpoint and intimidated even the most courageous of us all. Hate, literally, turned our world upside down! We have spent too much time under the most egregious influence and effect of hate. We have suffered enough apprehension, intimidation, and the fear of unknown kept us quiet and unconcerned for too long. We allowed segregation to become the norm rather than the exception.

We are now about to experience hate 2.0, and there is no better time to reject this enemy of man. The fact that violence is about to overtake our world, taking advantage of our I-don't-care-about-that attitude is a sign that our world is on the verge of highly destructive, elevated temperature, and there is no better time than now to stand up and say enough is enough. It is no longer against Africans, Jewish, and Hispanics. It is now against the entire human family. Look at Spain, France, Britain, and the United States to name a few.

The treatment received by Africa in the hands of those who decided to take advantage of her did not escape atrocity initiated and carried out by man. Her natural resources were removed against her will; and without due compensation, her glory tramped, her dignity diminished and stricken, her people killed for their natural resources. Africa became destitute, and her shining star replaced with everything negative. The "birthplace of the human family" became simply the "land of abject poverty, third world, filthy and no doubt, dark continent." Whatever remained of her people were felled into the category of "subhuman." They tried to smear Africans.

False and fake stories including a senseless research done by those who were eager to prove that God was wrong started to spread like inferno. Their ardent and extremely ambitious intent to reclassify and correct what God created, inspected, and certified as "good" quickly found allies among those willing to separate themselves from the rest. They did not hold back their effort to classify Africans as belonging to the family of "apes" and "gorillas" with "tails" among other things and no dignified habitat but treetops, swamps, and jungles.

Hate took over and the spirit of inclusiveness, and oneness varnished. Darkness and evil moved in with intent to permanent erase love, togetherness, and the brotherhood of man. We unsuspectingly inherited hate through blindly following the dictate of kings, queens, and their kingdoms. This laid the groundwork for hate group, their agenda, and shielded destructive division to emerge and exist. Confederate men and women saw an opportunity, grabbed it, and pushed it to its apex through intimidation, fear, and segregation.

PEACE WITH GOD

God is supposed to be in the center of religion—the one with exclusive right to our halleluiah, our loyalty and dedication. There should be no deviation from the original plan of God. A servant of God is expected to serve as the link between God and man, thereby talking to God, hearing from God, and delivering the unmistakable message of God. A servant of God is not expected to operate on theoretical knowledge built on hypothesis and possibilities but on unmistakable divine instructions established on untainted personal relationship with God.

Activities of a servant of God and his message to the people of God should not be affected by politics, social issues, or anything secular such as the concern for who is elected or appointed to serve in whatever capacity. Not only that, it should not be affected by insatiable desire for worldly affairs. Although there is nothing wrong in having ownership of a business capable of helping all of God's children while generating dependable income meant to glorify God. The only problem is when the desire to make the business successful at all costs totally ignores the will of God, insults intelligence through deceitful strategies without regard for the rule of law—constitutional and divine law. A servant of God is expected to recognize, appreciate, and encourage the children of God (regardless of ethnicity) without reservation and without prejudice. A servant of God is expected to be a reflection of God—in the world but not of the world.

All of the attributes of God provide us with a vivid picture of who God is as well as what we can expect from Him without injecting what we think is acceptable to God and without allowing our personal pride, culture, position, and the dictate of any board of directors to get in the way.

To know God is to know that He is a loving God, merciful God, omnipresent (He is everywhere) and unchangeable. "He is the same yesterday, today and tomorrow." Not only that, God is righteous, powerful, all knowing, and God is absolute truth. Don't let anybody fool you. God is righteous, holy, and no doubt, faithful and just. All these attributes tell us that God delights Himself in His creation.

We did not create God; He created us in His own image and for His glory. He is without beginning and without ending. As an all-powerful God. He does not need any human being to decide for Him or judge anyone in His name.

God is not afraid to make Himself as clear to us as possible. When Moses was not sure as to the source of the voice he heard, God quickly introduced Himself: "I am that I am." His mercy is everlasting, His power is unlimited, His love is ever flowing, His words never fail, and His presence can be felt from one end of the world to the other. You can hide from a fellow human being, but you are within the reach of the Almighty—no matter how high you go, always remember that God is still higher

If you think you are ordained by God to rid the world of unrighteousness, evil, and ungodliness, think again. God did not need you to inject wickedness into what belongs to Him. He simply requires you to love His people as much as He loves them, and that is your highest calling. "If a man says, I love God and hates his brother, he is a liar: for he that loves not his brother whom he hath seen, how can he love God whom he hath not seen?" (1 John 4:20).

CONSEQUENCES OF INACTION

System built on hate will continue to spew out hate unless something is done. We have lived with hate for a very long time, and it's beginning to look like the new norm. Accepting evil will do nothing but turn our world into the playground of evil. Two major attitudes are responsible for the unspeakable growth of hate:

1. Nonchalant attitude and lack of desire to stop hate.
2. Fear of acknowledging the source of hate.

If you see fire on your rooftop, it is not a good idea to ignore it simply because you think rain is on its way. The do-nothing attitude of the children of light will equally do nothing but encourage imperturbable reaction guaranteed to lead to incomprehensible and never-ending suffering among the children of God. Apathy is the devil's way of convincing the children of light to stay away; therefore find something, worthwhile and rewarding to do with your time because this problem is too big and too complicated to tackle.

Division and discrimination carefully and methodically cultivated were forcefully delivered through fear, threat, and intimidation. Many unsuspecting men and women, through passive attitude, helped nurtured it for these many years. Those who could have put out this kind of fierce fire of hate appeared less concerned because of the fact that they are not affected by it. If anything, they became the beneficiaries of what could have gone to the shutouts. It boosted their egos and gave them exclusive right convenient and uplifting.

NONCHALANT ATTITUDE AND LACK OF DESIRE TO STOP HATE

Why would you want to stick your neck out for something that started over 250 years ago? Why would you want to disrupt your peaceful, quiet, and somewhat-rewarding life? Not only that, the most personal question most people would like to ask is, "What is in this for me anyway?" These are some of often dismissing questions usually from most people who are angry at history that was originally written with intent to deceive and no plan to correct all the misrepresentations of the past.

There is nothing more pleasing to oppressor than the silent voice of the oppressed. The indifferent attitude of the oppressed is grease that keeps the oppressive engine running. It is even better if the oppressed can be pacified by crumbs. To say that hate along with all its destructive elements such as discrimination, prejudice, segregation, etc., is going to vanish and that "the situation will eventually take care of itself" without the tireless effort of people willing to stop it is like living in perpetual state of a never-ending daydreaming. Without the diligence, and at times desire of those willing to agitate the sleep of evil, hate will continue to grow, and true integration without demeaning label along with constant reminder of "You are different from us" will continue to have the last say in our world.

If a highly educated, intelligent, and democratically elected president of the United States can be ridiculed because of the color of his skin and a hardworking athlete who rose to the top of his game on excellent skills and pure merit can be lampooned and ridiculed, believe me, we cannot afford to give up and say, "It doesn't matter." If peaceful protest can lead to loss of life in the hand of determined hate group, it is difficult to look the other way. If the man elected as the president, expected to lead, can ignite negative feelings toward those who are simply exercising their right to protest for right by calling them "sons of bitches" on national television, it is difficult to not do anything.

FEAR OF ACKNOWLEDGING THE SOURCE OF HATE

One of the most potent enemies of man is intimidation. It is capable of slowly and softly paralyzing the mind with a never-ending sense of guilt and defeat. It always come with a do-nothing attitude that is extremely counterproductive. Intimidation is a killing agent meant for the coward and timid. Intimidation is capable of creating distance between people. It can damage personality, thereby forcing the intimidated to start behaving differently from the rest of the human family

We cannot afford not to call hate what it is—enemy of the human family. If we are only concerned about what is convenient, politically correct, and beneficial, we are in a way creating an environment where hate is allowed to grow with no consequences, whatsoever. On the other hand, if we allow God to be glorified in our lives through our service to Him, we are bound to experience the goodness of the Lord even in the land of the living. "If only in this world we have hope, we are of all men the most miserable."

NONVIOLENCE OR NONEXISTENCE

We've come a long way to allow selfishness and greed to divide us. There is no better way to end this volume of *Culprit of Division* than to invoke the word of the man who once called himself an "extremist for peace" and "a drum major for justice." Dr. King believed that humanity had two choices: "nonviolence or nonexistence." Regardless of whether you agree with the story of the past in the interest of suppressing facts, what is true can never be erased.

The time to defuse and deescalate is now. The road to complete healing is not in holier-than-thou attitude. The road to healing is not in the effort to try and shame one segment of the society into believing that it only happened to them. Victims of heinous crime of rape, for the most part, usually feels better when they are made aware of the fact that they are not alone and is not their fault. Those who are suffering from mental illness (of any kind) are usually able to deal with the stigma associated with mental illness when they know that the problem of mental illness is not unique to them. Those who are wrestling with serious medical issues need to be reassured about the fact that it had happened to the best of us. Knowing that you are not the only one ever affected by whatever problem or stigmas can set you on the way to faster psychological and even physical recovery.

Those who are affected by the ugliness of the past need to boldly step forward and acknowledge their dilemma! Slavery is not unique to African Americans alone. We can agree to disagree the truth is already out and supported by suppressed but never disputed or destroyed history, laws and executive actions. A lot of black people came here as explorers and sojourners, as free men and women and some were brought here because of slave trade. A lot of Irish and some English men and women came here as a result of slave trade and also as "servants." We can all accept that fact and unanimously deal with the shameful stories of the past in the interest of equality and peaceful coexistence. The holier-than-thou attitude is not in the best interest of unity and definitely not the right way to deal with divisiveness.

The desire to claim "first to discover" and the blatant disregard for the effort of those who came before led to false claims of kings and their kingdoms' selfish intentions. Joshua could have denied those who went before him to see the promise land; it would have made his voyage less believable and cast a never-ending shadow of doubt on his effort. Instead, he acknowledged what took place, and the whole story came out more credible than we can ever imagine. The fact that many noble men and women had been to this land now known as the Americas before Christopher Columbus is undeniable. The fact that this land belongs to all of us who labored so hard for it and died for it is carved in stone! The fact that the shameful story of slavery affected blacks as well as white is unfortunately true. We can either acknowledge all of what took place or deny them; the facts can never be obliterated. What is more important right now is where do we go from here?

Many of those unscientific studies and false explanation concerning our differences are designed to create inequality. Many of the effort of some so-called scientist designed to validate divisive and unfounded findings along with irrelevant public opinion are nothing but just too discriminating and segregating efforts designed to legitimize lies. There is no blue blood, black blood, but red blood in all of us. We are all members of the same human family with all of us connected in one way or another to the "birth place of mankind"—Africa. Better yet, we all have the breath of God in our lungs, and there is no greater binding tie! The truth is out and can never be swept under the rug, suppressed, or denied.

We can go after one another with the intent to wipe away one another or bury the truth in our bid for false superiority and supremacy that will do nothing but continue to create a never-ending gulf of inequality and separation between us.

What kind of explanation is there to justify a rally organized by a militant group fully equipped with guns, clubs, knives, and even Molotov cocktail while shouting, "We want out streets back, we want our cities back. Jews will not replace us!" How can anyone come to the conclusion that these are "nice people"? Like I said earlier, to believe that those are nice people is to show moral deficiency requiring immediate attention. What do these militant groups need to realize that intimidation and hate will never solve a problem of this magnitude?

The other side, the counterprotesters, organized peaceful protest to show their resentment to injustice, hate, and segregation. They came with placards and Bibles. They came with the intent to use their presence as a deterrent. They came to speak for the disadvantaged, the oppressed, and the marginalized. They came to show that hate has no place in our society. They came to let America know that the days of cross burning and lynching in the middle of the night are over.

We can choose to focus on what is good in all of us, come together in the interest of a better relationship, or we can choose to continue in the same destructive path the confederacy made available about 150 years ago. The choice is ours. If ever there was a time we dropped this rate race, now is the time.

Two days prior to Saturday, September 30, 2017, evil descended on Las Vegas to unleash his premeditated, preplanned, carefully crafted, and methodically orchestrated fury. To imagine this type of massacre carried out by a privileged individual—professional person by all means with access to all the good things of life—defies logic.

Stephen Paddock, an individual stockpiling ammunitions including many semiautomatic arsenal along with bump stock—a modification devices (gun accessory needed to increase firing power) capable of making those semiautomatic weapons work like fully automatic weapons. This individual had forty-seven weapons in his possession. Why is all that necessary? Why would anyone need forty-seven different guns for protection? Is this an indication that we see one another as enemies and not as fellow citizens with differences—political, philosophical, and ideological?

Stephen Paddock took residence in the Mandalay Bay and was able to modify his surroundings to include surveillance system. He also came with enough bump stocks, which helped him to successfully modify the weapons employed to take the lives of many innocent people. Those who came to enjoy a well-deserved weekend of relaxation and fun did not know that they were walking into death trap. The attacker, Stephen Paddock, the man who killed 58 people and injured approximately 489 in one night did not leave a clue as to his motives before taking his own life. No manifesto discovered.

There was no known connection to terror group, domestic or foreign. No antigovernment view or agenda discovered, and no significant discontent of any kind revealed. As reported by Roland Oliphant of the *Telegraph*, "Next to his body, police found an arsenal of weapons including more than ten rifles but no immediate clue telling them what drove him to open fire from his window at the concert goers below." If the ultimate goal was for evil triumphant, it has failed miserably.

The good people of the United States stepped up to save the wounded. Even in the face of danger, children of God did not allow fear and the desire to run for their lives to push them away from those badly injured and in need of help. A lot of people later stepped up with the desire to donate blood in the interest of saving more lives. This act of kindness did not discriminate. The recipients couldn't care less if the blood given to save them from dying was from a Jewish person, Asian, European, African, or black or white. The goal was to save lives. Human family rose up to the occasion and came together as members of the same and only one race—the human race. Evil did not win.

The most important thing here was all about saving humanity—this is all about doing God's will. Hate, as alluded to in this book, "is too great a burden to bear." Dr. King emphasized that "darkness cannot put out darkness; only light can do that." Those who gave part of themselves are in a way allowing their lights to drown out the darkness of hate. What we need in this day and age is for children of God to continue to allow the illuminating light of God to drive out darkness from this world.

The root of our discord cannot be ignored. Truth about the real story of our existence must be told. It can no longer be denied, suppressed, or pushed into oblivion. It must be told exactly the way it happened. The only effort required is to comfort one another with our testimonies and make conscientious effort to wipe away any mentioning of the words *slaves* and *slavery* in reference to any ethnic group or in reference to the human family. We cannot afford not to deal with the main problem. Sugarcoating will do nothing but deepen the existing divide.

There should be no place in our society for any kind of hate—concealed hate or gratuitous hate and most especially label-induced hate and all forms of hate. This should not be allowed to ever flourish within the human family.

ABOUT THE AUTHOR

Dr. Henry I. Balogun is the chairman/CEO of MedNet Healthcare Systems Inc. and also founder/CEO of www.ClinicTools.org—complete clinical management platform for behavioral health, psychiatric, and psychological services establishments.

Dr. Balogun, a former teacher at the Bucks County Community College in Pennsylvania, is also the founder/CEO of www.PrimeHangout. com. Feel free to log in to www.PrimeHangout.com to become a registered user or watch his video explaining what PrimeHangout is all about.

He is also a published author of *Beyond Cut, Copy and Paste*, as well as *Microsoft Office for Healthcare Professionals* including *Culprit of Division*.

BLURB

Our world is seeded with landmine of hate, moral deficiencies, inequalities, and collaboration with evil! The greatest enemy of the human race, a major roadblock to genuine integration, equality, and peaceful coexistence is hate and the spread of it.

www.ingramcontent.com/pod-product-compliance
Lightning Source LLC
Chambersburg PA
CBHW070656290526
45790CB00001B/350